Encouraging *Words* to Live By

365 DAYS OF HOPE FOR THE ANXIOUS AND OVERWHELMED

Anne Costa

Published by The Word Among Us Press
7115 Guilford Drive, Suite 100
Frederick, Maryland 21704
wau.org

23 22 21 20 19   1 2 3 4 5

ISBN: 978-1-59325-344-8
eISBN: 978-1-59325-517-6

Cover design by Faceout Studios
Interior design by Suzanne Earl

Made and printed in the United States of America

Library of Congress Control Number: 2019939493

For my beautiful daughter, Mary Grace,

my reason for being.

CONTENTS

JANUARY

JANUARY 1

"Behold, your mother."
John 19:27

The heart of Mary never sleeps. We can entrust everything to her, knowing that even God did the same!

Give her everything that is too heavy for you to carry. Tell her your hopes and dreams for the coming year. If you don't know how to pray, let her carry your unspoken wishes to the sanctuary of the sacred heart of her Son. St. Louis de Montfort said that "if you put all the love of all the mothers into one heart, it still would not equal the love of the Heart of Mary for her children."[1] We can trust her and find comfort in knowing that her love covers all and cannot fail.

Lord, sustain me through the beautiful heart of your mother.

JANUARY 2

I am with you and will protect you wherever you go. . . . I will never leave you until I have done what I promised you.
Genesis 28:15

Scripture overflows with accounts of how God delivers on his promises in a big way. Our vision is limited by our humanity, but God's divine plan for each one of us is rich with promise. He is fully capable of bringing about our highest good, but it means that we must step aside and let him lead the way. We can stand before him with our hands outstretched in a gesture of hope and surrender as we await whatever he wants to give us.

Lord, I open myself to your promise and possibility.

JANUARY 3

Our help is in the name of the LORD.
Psalm 124:8

There is power in the name of Jesus! Invoking his name is a prayer in itself. To reinforce our understanding of this devotion, the Church has established January 3rd as the feast of the Holy Name of Jesus. Scripture offers many examples of how the name of Jesus has saved souls (see Acts 4:12), cast out demons (see Luke 10:17), and cured bodily and spiritual ills (see Acts 4:30). Proverbs 18:10 says, "The name of the LORD is a strong tower; / the just run to it and are safe."

How many times in your life have you cried out "Jesus" without really knowing what to say next? Today we are reminded that nothing more is needed.

Jesus, holy is your name.

JANUARY 4

He said to them, "Come, and you will see."
John 1:39

Imagine walking along a road with Jesus. Look into his eyes. Can you see the light? Can you see the compassion and safety that he offers? When Jesus says, "You will see," it means that he has something to show you.

Jesus wants us to be open to a different vision of ourselves and our lives. He wants us to be able to see ourselves as he sees us—as God's beloved. You are complete and beautiful in the eyes of our Father. You don't have to earn God's love. All you have to do is follow Jesus and keep the eyes of your heart open to what he wants to reveal to you, one day at a time.

Dear Jesus, show me.

JANUARY 5

Beloved, if [our] hearts do not condemn us,
we have confidence in God.
1 John 3:21

Our hearts were made to be filled with love, not condemnation. How we talk to ourselves—the messages we send—can either feed or starve our souls. We shouldn't let our own inner chatter drown out the voice of God, who is love.

Confidence in God comes from knowing him and recognizing his voice. God's love language is best heard in the quiet confines of our hearts. Let the condemning thoughts die down like a distant echo and allow the whisper of the One who loves you fill your listening heart.

Beloved Lord, speak and breathe confidence in me.

JANUARY 6

Arise! Shine, for your light has come,
the glory of the LORD has dawned upon you.
Isaiah 60:1

A woman stepped out in faith, but she was fearful, so she asked the Lord for a sign. She went on with her day, business as usual, until the skies opened up and it started to rain. An ordinary day turned into an extraordinary experience of peace when a rainbow appeared and seemed to follow her for miles and miles until she reached her destination.

On this feast of the Epiphany, remember that God delights in revealing himself to us in unexpected ways and is ready to shine his glory upon us. Those who seek him will always find him.

Lord, send me a sign.

JANUARY 7

Whoever possesses the Son has life.
1 John 5:12

Jesus allows himself to be possessed by us. In Holy Communion, he dissolves into our being, consumed as the bread of our lives.

Receiving Jesus in the Eucharist provides the nourishment we need for our souls. Through him and in him, we find the grace and power to grow spiritually as we become more like him day by day. The more open we are to this grace, the more we expect in faith to receive it, the more Jesus can take possession of our hearts and minds to bring us peace.

His embrace offers us the greatest possible freedom. We don't have to fear getting close to him. He is trustworthy, gentle, and life-giving.

Lord, possess me.

JANUARY 8

For my thoughts are not your thoughts,
nor are your ways my ways.
Isaiah 55:8

God can take what doesn't make sense, or seem fair, and bring about a blessing. As she dealt with her illness, my friend with cancer discovered an inner strength that she never knew she had. A man who lost his sight discovered a vision for how he was to help others with similar challenges. Another man, who lost everything because of a poor financial decision, packed up and moved to another part of the country. There he met his wife and raised a beautiful family. He would never have had those blessings without that financial setback.

What a comfort it is to know that God's ways are not like ours, but better!

Lord, help me to love your ways, even when I don't under-
stand them.

JANUARY 9

"In truth, I see that God shows no partiality."
Acts 10:34

You are God's favorite and so am I! As his beloved sons and daughters, we don't have to compete for his attention or clamor for his love. We don't have to worry that we will be passed over, overshadowed, or fail to receive what we need from him.

In this family of God, there is no need to be jealous. We all have a place, and we all have a purpose. We are free to encourage one another and share in our abundant inheritance together. There are enough goodness and grace to go around.

Lord, I claim my special place in your heart.

JANUARY 10

I delight to do your will, my God;
your law is in my inner being.
Psalm 40:9

The psalms are the beautiful hymns of Scripture, most of them attributed to David, who is said to have suffered from anxiety and depression. He is one of us! In Psalm 40, he reminds us that God's law is within our hearts.

What comfort it is to know that God's will and his ways are so close to us that he is a source of guidance from *within* our own hearts! We don't have to go on a great quest or play a guessing game with God. As we practice holy listening through prayer, we will recognize his presence and the way that we should go.

Lord, reveal your ways from within.

JANUARY 11

There is no fear in love, but perfect love drives out fear.
1 John 4:18

St. Margaret Mary Alacoque enjoyed almost continuous interior dialogue with Jesus. Beginning in 1673, he revealed his sacred heart to her in a series of visions, and she began to promote the devotion to the Sacred Heart of Jesus that we know today. Her writings offer great hope and encouragement, directing us to focus entirely on the heart of Jesus and his promise to bring us peace, refuge, and strength. She wrote,

> Should you find yourself overwhelmed by fear, cast yourself into the abyss of the unshaken confidence of the Sacred Heart, and there your fear will give place to love . . . Go to the Sacred Heart and draw from It the strength which will invigorate and revive you.[2]

Lord, to combat fear, today I will enter the sanctuary of your Sacred Heart from which all love flows.

JANUARY 12

Are my tears not stored in your flask,
recorded in your book?
Psalm 56:9

Grief is a doorway to your deepest self, so let the tears flow. God counts and collects them and makes note of every one of them. Our tears matter to him. They are meant to wash clean the debris that collects in our souls; their salt purifies all that keeps us from knowing his peace and comfort. If we do not allow the tears, then we cannot let him in to ease the pain and calm the fears of the inner storms that plague us.

Lord, receive my tears.

JANUARY 13

"Those who are well do not need a physician,
but the sick do."
Mark 2:17

We do not have to "clean up" to be helped by Jesus. Even in our sickness, he only sees the goodness and potential within us. His focus is always on making us well. One of the best places to receive the healing balm of our Holy Physician is in the Sacrament of Reconciliation. There he applies his mercy to our ailing minds, hearts, and souls.

As the master diagnostician, he can root out the causes of our stress, replace our fears, and set us on course toward wholeness in him. It's OK to need him. We all do.

Lord, heal me.

JANUARY 14

"Speak, for your servant is listening."
1 Samuel 3:10

Listening is an act of love. If you are fortunate enough to have a friend who knows how to listen, you have certainly found a treasure. An active listener values and cherishes the inner reality of another person enough to refrain from judging, evaluating, or formulating a response. Such a listener seeks the complete message, even beyond the words that are being spoken.

Focus, engagement, reflection, and response are the sacred movements that make up a listening encounter. So consider: are you an active listener where Jesus is concerned? When he speaks to you in prayer, at Mass, and while reading the Scriptures, are you truly listening?

Holy Spirit, teach me how to listen.

JANUARY 15

"So do not be afraid; you are worth
more than many sparrows."
Matthew 10:31

What we achieve or accomplish is not who we are. Our value does not come from what we do. Let God reveal to you, moment by moment and layer by layer, how precious you are to him, just as you are. We do not have to perform; we do not have to excel; we do not have to earn his love.

Receive the security of his love. Rest in him and know that you do not have to prove your worth to God. You are of inestimable value, a treasure in his sight.

Lord, help me to know my worth.

JANUARY 16

The LORD answered, I myself will go along, to give you rest.
Exodus 33:14

God is deeply concerned with our rest, both physically and spiritually. Our souls find a holy rest in detachment from the world, a state of being that we can pray for and practice.

Disconnecting from the clamor around us is the first step. We need to turn down the volume of our lives and plug into a peaceful experience, whether it be through reading a book, listening to soothing music, watching a sunset, or engaging in a deep and thoughtful conversation. This type of activity settles us in our spirit, but still engages us in something that will fill us up with the things of God.

Lord, bring a holy rest to my soul.

JANUARY 17

*Whatever is true, whatever is honorable, whatever is just,
whatever is pure, whatever is lovely, whatever is gracious,
if there is any excellence and if there is anything worthy of
praise, think about these things.*

Philippians 4:8

O ur thoughts are our possessions. We own them. We choose them. We can control what we focus our minds on at any given moment. We can direct our attention to what we choose, raise our awareness about our choices, and keep track of what we are thinking and why we are thinking it. A great deal of what we think about all day long is habitual and may not serve us well. It's time to take an inventory: what are you thinking?

Lord, I lift my thoughts to you.

JANUARY 18

*With my own voice I will call out to the L*ORD*,*
and he will answer me from his holy mountain.
Psalm 3:5

Can I make a case for "long miracles"? We often want instantaneous results when we pray, and spontaneous healings from our problems, but perhaps we don't receive these because we can't handle them all at once. When I tell people that I prayed for nine years to be free of specific fears, they lament that it took so long. Yet I look back and realize that Jesus used those years to teach me so much about him and his heart.

If I had been healed instantaneously, I would not have the deep, abiding, and trusting relationship that I have with Jesus today. The fact that it took many years before I was freed from my fears does not make my healing any less a miracle. But Jesus knew that time would be an essential ingredient if those wounds were to be healed for good.

Lord, help me to accept your healing action
in my life as it comes.

JANUARY 19

"What do you want me to do for you?"
Luke 18:41

What can Jesus do for you today? He asked the blind man that same question in the Gospel of Luke. He knew what the man wanted—just as he knows what we want—but sometimes it is good for us to speak out loud what is in our hearts. Giving voice to our deepest desires sets us on the road to fulfilling them. Acknowledging our needs helps us take the first steps toward finding ways to meet our needs. In the same way, when we articulate our fears, sharing them with someone else, they lose their power over us.

Don't be afraid to say it out loud. God is always listening.

Lord, I need _____*.*

JANUARY 20

"In the world you will have trouble, but take courage, I have conquered the world."
John 16:33

Courage is not the absence of fear, but the willingness to act in spite of it. We will never be completely free of fear because it is often necessary to warn us of danger or to signal a need for a change. We will still encounter trouble in this world, but with Jesus we know that eventually we will emerge victorious.

Courageous people can be fragile, wounded, worried, or weary. But they will always choose good and do the right thing, no matter what the cost. Even in the face of contempt, rejection, or ridicule, courageous people carry on.

Lord, fill me with courage today and always.

JANUARY 21

"Behold, I make all things new. "
Revelations 21:5

Letting go is a lifelong endeavor. Releasing our pain or disappointment over the way things should have been can take time. Yet we can't truly move on until we do. Letting go of regret and guilt takes patience; we need to be compassionate toward ourselves. Even good things might need to pass away to make room for the rebirth that God wants to bring about within us.

Sometimes our fears are a force of resistance, inhibiting the newness and spiritual springtime that are still to come.

Lord, help me let go.

JANUARY 22

I praise you, because I am wonderfully made.
Psalm 139:14

Many of us need healing in our relationship with our bodies. First comes awareness.

Pay attention to the inner dialogue that you carry on about your body. Are you nourishing your body with good and accepting thoughts and respectful language, or are you hypercritical and self-rejecting?

Next comes action. Are you treating your body to regular exercise, healthy food, and proper rest? What one practice can you take up that will communicate honor and embrace self-care for your body as the amazing masterpiece that it is?

The *Catechism of the Catholic Church* states that the body and soul are one (see 365). That means that what we do to our bodies, we do to our souls. Let's practice kindness toward both.

Lord, heal me, body and soul.

JANUARY 23

*Let your love for one another be intense, because love covers
a multitude of sins.*
1 Peter 4:8

Surrendering to love is a moment-to-moment spiritual battle. When we decide to love, no matter what, we can come face-to-face with our unspoken fears of betrayal or rejection.

It is easy to love "everybody," but not so easy to love the person sitting across from you at the kitchen table or in the boardroom. When we get up close and personal with people, we also get acquainted with their "multitude of sins," and they, in turn, are exposed to our own. Loving constantly gets a bit harder then.

Yet if we want true peace in our lives, love is our only choice. Applying love to every encounter can never lead us astray. If you have tried everything else, try love.

*Lord, I need your grace to love constantly.
Infuse me with it now!*

JANUARY 24

The LORD, your God, is in your midst, / a mighty savior, / Who will rejoice over you with gladness, / and renew you in his love, / Who will sing joyfully because of you.
Zephaniah 3:17

For many of us, the roots of rejection run deep. We carry holes in our souls that long to be filled, and wounds from the past that cry out to be lanced. Our own families can let us down, leaving us feeling like a stranger even in their midst.

But remember that you are never far from your Father's heart. You are a member of his family forever, and he delights in you. He will never reject you or stop loving you. You make his heart sing!

Father God, I am grateful to be your child.

JANUARY 25

A king is not saved by a great army,
nor a warrior delivered by great strength.
Psalm 33:16

Edith Stein—St. Teresa Benedicta of the Cross—was a Jew in Hitler's Germany, a brilliant philosopher, and a university professor who converted to Catholicism and became a Carmelite nun. In spite of her intellectual and spiritual advantages, she discovered the quiet exhilaration and freedom that come from knowing one's limitations. She said this: "The knowledge of my limits has made great strides. . . . This knowledge does not depress me."[3]

We all have limitations, and we will all reach our limit at one point or another. When we do, it's OK to say, "I can't" or "I don't want to right now." But no one can know what your limits are unless you tell them. Being clear about what you can and cannot do can go a long way in reducing stress and anxiety.

Lord, I can't. Amen.

JANUARY 26

Your every act should be done with love.
1 Corinthians 16:14

St. Teresa of Cacutta said, "We can do no great things; only small things with great love."[4] This puts everything into perspective, doesn't it? It takes the pressure off and tempers the temptation to overachieve in order to leave a good impression with others.

When we do things out of love, we are set free from the bondage of doing things to earn the approval of others. It no longer matters what everybody else thinks of us. We are free to love others and ourselves just as we are.

Letting God's love sink into our minds and hearts is a full-time occupation. Putting our energy into receiving his love instead of trying to achieve earthly gain can bring us great interior peace. He heals us with his love so that we can do small things with that love, one day at a time.

Lord, let me love you in my littleness.

JANUARY 27

"You shall love the Lord your God with all your heart,
with all your soul, with all your mind,
and with all your strength."
Mark 12:30

Giving God first place in our hearts can be a struggle. We relegate him to a lower rank for all sorts of reasons—we have our minigods and motivations that steer us away from his heart. We can also let worries seep in and crowd him out. If you have evicted God from his rightful place in the center of your life, invite him back in.

It's never too late, and we can never love God too much.

God, come home to my heart.

JANUARY 28

We love because he first loved us.
1 John 4:19

God's love is a wellspring, the origin of all love. The mystery of his love is worth contemplating from time to time, because without it, none of us would be here. Some people experience God's love most keenly in nature, others at the foot of the cross or in Adoration. We all experience God's love when we are on the receiving end of love from someone else or when we are sharing our love for another.

We never love alone. God is always within our love, sharing himself abundantly so that you and I can experience just a taste of what is yet to come.

God, I love your love.

JANUARY 29

Then let us no longer judge one another, but rather
resolve never to put a stumbling block or hindrance
in the way of a brother.
Romans 14:13

Proving a point at all costs is very costly. As we lead the charge to be understood, we close the door on a conversation that could lead to greater understanding. Relationships require mutual respect, and we have a responsibility to truly hear others, even when we totally disagree with them.

Disagreement should not mean disdain or dismissal. We can let go of the need to change another person's mind. We can simply let the differences of opinion float to the surface and be carried away downstream.

Shift your focus from making a point to making a true connection.

Lord, help me let it go.

JANUARY 30

Honor one another above yourselves.
Romans 12:10 (NIV)

When we realize that we don't have to be in first place all the time, we take a lot of pressure off ourselves. We can shift the attention from our needs and worries and focus instead on building up others. This is a sure way to reduce anxiety. Making other people happy and affirming their worth and goodness can cure what ails us. Love heals. Every little thing we can do to decrease so that Jesus can increase his love in us will bring us peace and satisfaction. Try it.

Lord, give me the grace to honor others above myself.

JANUARY 31

But I shall show you a still more excellent way.
1 Corinthians 12:31

We have a "road map" for the excellent way of love in the following passage:

Love is patient, love is kind.
It is not jealous, [love] is not pompous,
it is not inflated, it is not rude,
it does not seek its own interests,
it is not quick-tempered, it does not brood over injury,
it does not rejoice over wrongdoing
but rejoices with the truth.
It bears all things, believes all things,
hopes all things, endures all things.
Love never fails. (1 Corinthians 13:4-8)

The Lord is our shepherd and our teacher in the way of love. Let the way of love be your greatest ambition and accomplishment.

Lord, teach me to love.

FEBRUARY

FEBRUARY 1

*In all circumstances give thanks, for this is the will of God
for you in Christ Jesus.*
1 Thessalonians 5:18

Gratitude lifts us and gifts us with an abiding joy. It is balm
for an anxious spirit. Thanking God in the middle of
our trials releases a power to overcome fear; it's an antidote
to stress. God calls us to gratitude because he knows that it
is good for us. A habit of thankfulness will help us to release
negative thoughts and emotions and replace them with a slow
burning peace that seeps into our hearts, regardless of the
storms that swirl around us.

Thank you, Lord!

FEBRUARY 2

"And you yourself a sword will pierce."
Luke 2:35

During what should have been a joyous occasion—the presentation of her child at the Temple—Mary received some ominous news. Simeon's prophecy pointed directly to a future certainty of sorrow. We all face something similar in our lifetimes. The loss of a loved one, the sting of betrayal, disappointment, an unexpected diagnosis—these are all impending possibilities. We cannot spend our lives trying to ward off suffering. If we do, we will not be living at all. The best gift we can give ourselves is to learn how to live in the present moment. Right now, we can relax. This minute, we can breathe in joy. Right now, we can rest at the altar of the present moment and live.

Lord, thank you for this present moment.

FEBRUARY 3

Trust in the LORD with all your heart,
on your own intelligence do not rely.
Proverbs 3:5

When I don't have answers, I remind myself that, as St. John Henry Newman wrote, "[God] knows what he is about."[5] One way to give up control is to sit with our questions for a while. It's not easy—we often grow restless and demanding, seeking a solution before its time. We want a directive or an explanation; we search for signs, but none come. Consolations dry up, prayers seemingly go unanswered, and all attempts at figuring things out may fail—but still, God knows what he's about.

God, gratefully I lean on you.

FEBRUARY 4

"Do not let your hearts be troubled or afraid."
John 14:27

When Mary said, "May it be done to me according to your word" (Luke 1:38), her surrender was lifelong and complete. In this surrender, her heart and mind found total serenity. We can follow her example and find the same.

Letting go and letting God are daily commitments in the spiritual life. We can accumulate many harmful attitudes as we go through life: grudges, fears, insecurities, self-condemning thoughts, to name several. We will need to let go of these in order to heal and receive the peace that God wants to give us. God is God, but he waited for Mary's permission before he fulfilled his plan. She had to consent to his perfect will, and so do we.

Lord, be it done to me according to your word.

FEBRUARY 5

On the way of wisdom I direct you.
Proverbs 4:11

Walking through the gate of wisdom leads us into the garden of joy.

Wisdom is a gift of the Holy Spirit that enables us to know and love the things of God above all things. It permits his divine truth to penetrate our hearts, filling us with joy. Wisdom tempers anxiety because through it we are able to form appropriate attachments and establish healthy boundaries. Through wisdom we can set our spiritual priorities straight and find the blessing of balance. God will always answer any prayer for an increase of wisdom.

Lord, make me wise.

FEBRUARY 6

"For my yoke is easy, and my burden light."
Matthew 11:30

Just about every time I complained or whined about something as a child, my mother would say, "God never promised you a rose garden!" It used to make me really mad, of course, but now that I'm grown, I have come to realize something about that statement. It's entirely true: God never promised me a rose garden—he's promised me *so much more.*

Deeper moments of joy, greater abundance, and a blossoming of faith have followed every period of trial in my life. God has lavished me with more beauty, more goodness, and more to be grateful for than I could have ever imagined—and it has not been in spite of the trials, but because of them.

If you are going through difficult times right now, hold fast to the promises of God; they are in bloom all around you, and they are more beautiful than the most perfect rose.

God's got this.

Lord, I claim your promises!

FEBRUARY 7

Thanks be to God for his indescribable gift!
2 Corinthians 9:15

God wants to bless you today. He wants to raise your heart and mind to new heights, up above the clouds. When your plane takes off on an overcast and stormy day, it's always amazing to ascend through the clouds and be greeted with glorious sunshine! It's a good reminder that our storms are temporary, and God is a constant source of beauty and light, even when we can't quite see it. His constant glory is always present, and his life, love, and mercy are always flowing from heaven to earth. During every Mass, we are reminded of this ever-flowing source of grace.

We can receive his good gifts at any time. Be open. Be expectant. God never stops giving.

Lord, thank you for your generous heart.

FEBRUARY 8

"Ask, and it will be given to you; seek and you will find;
knock and the door will be opened to you."
Matthew 7:7

Ask the Lord to speak to you today, and then fully expect to hear him through the people, places, and circumstances of your life. When you go to church, welcome his true presence, and wait for his word to speak to your heart. If you cannot receive him sacramentally, you can pray this prayer:

My Jesus,
I believe that You
are present in the most Holy Sacrament.
I love You above all things,
and I desire to receive You into my soul.
Since I cannot at this moment
receive You sacramentally,
come at least spiritually into my heart.
I embrace You as if You were already there
and unite myself wholly to You.
Never permit me to be separated from You. Amen.[6]

Lord, always be near.

FEBRUARY 9

The LORD's acts of mercy are not exhausted,
his compassion is not spent;
They are renewed each morning.
Lamentations 3:22-23

Every sunrise is a reminder of God's faithfulness. If you are carrying a burden or resentment from yesterday, let it go. It's a new day and a clean slate for you and everyone you will encounter today. We have twenty-four hours of opportunities, possibilities, and new beginnings before us. Today's Scripture verse confirms this: God's mercy, care, and compassion are renewed each morning.

He is a Father who never gets tired, worn out, or distracted. We are surrounded by the beauty of his creation and sustained by his endless love. As the day unfolds, remember to look out the window or step outside and offer a short prayer of thanks for the lovely earthly home that God has given us. Praise him for the way he reveals himself to us through the natural world.

Heavenly Father, thank you for your
endless, beautiful beginnings.

FEBRUARY 10

"I have heard your prayer;
I have seen your tears.
Now I am healing you."
2 Kings 20:5

We all need to be freed or healed in one way or another, and Jesus is still in the business of healing and deliverance. We may not recognize the healing force of Jesus because it is often gradual, unfolding in a way that extracts the best fruit from our struggles.

Our job is to cooperate with his grace, not resist it. We remain honest with him about our feelings and we release our fears to the best of our ability as we wait in joyful hope for the coming of our Savior. This is the way of healing.

Lord, heal and deliver me.

FEBRUARY 11

"Take care, then, that the light in you not become darkness."
Luke 11:35

Your light reflects the presence of God in you—those you encounter should be able to see that light. The enemy of our souls would like us to hide our light under a bushel basket, but God has other plans. For years and years, I was afraid to let my light shine. I had a false sense of humility about this, but I also had let darkness have the upper hand in certain areas of my life. Gratefully, I found my way to the One who is light in the sacrament of healing known as Confession.

Your light is your responsibility. How are you tending to it? What do you need to do so that the glow of God's presence continues within you?

Lord, let there be light.

FEBRUARY 12

A person will reap only what he sows.
Galatians 6:7

If you give joy, you get it back. Joy is contagious, and it's a beautiful blessing when we reap a harvest of joy in our hearts. We can make a daily decision to sow joy in our interaction with others.

To increase the measure of joy in our lives, we need to turn down the volume on complaining, criticism, and catastrophic thinking. Those three deadly Cs are the greatest killjoys of all. Let's replace them with seeds of encouragement for others, genuine compliments, and gestures of heartfelt concern. If we do this, we'll watch joy grow in our own life and theirs.

Lord, I choose joy.

FEBRUARY 13

And Mary kept all these things,
reflecting on them in her heart.
Luke 2:19

Go within. God lives there, deep inside you. There is a reservoir within your soul, a treasure trove of tranquility and grace. It is a well that never runs dry, awaiting your return. Your outside world will change when you reconnect with what is within you.

This interior space needs constant attention and care. If we nurture the silence within, tending the garden of our hearts, we will produce much fruit. Mary shows us the way. Her pondering, still hidden, continues to this day.

Mary, accompany me.

FEBRUARY 14

A friend is a friend at all times.
Proverbs 17:17

Even Jesus needed companions when he walked this earth. None of us can go it alone. When it came time for Jesus to face his death, he made sure to let his disciples know that he called them friends. This lends such importance to the gift of friendship. He went so far as to say, "No one has greater love than this, to lay down one's life for one's friends." (John 15:13).

If you have been hurt by friends or have trouble making or keeping them, ask Jesus to send you some godly, good friends. He never fails to answer this prayer. Jesus valued friendship, and he wants us to enjoy one another in friendship and love.

Lord, send me a good friend.

FEBRUARY 15

"For I know well the plans I have in mind for you—
*[declares] the L*ORD*—plans for your welfare and not for*
woe, so as to give you a future of hope."
Jeremiah 29:11

A popular saying reminds us that a head full of fears has no space for dreams. Today's verse reminds me that God himself has dreams for me. Not only that, but my entire future is in his hands. If this is true, then what do I have to fear? Today, let's trust in God's dreams for us and ask him about them in prayer. Release your fears into his capable hands and dream.

Lord, show me.

FEBRUARY 16

*"I came so that they might have life
and have it more abundantly."*
John 10:10

There is a state of peak performance known as flow. When we're in a "flow state," we're energized, focused, completely involved, and fully immersed in whatever we're doing. We're "in the zone," as flow is also known.[7]

On the spiritual journey, we call this living the abundant life, or walking in the Spirit. This is not so much a state to be achieved as it is an experience to enter into through silence, prayer, and a daily commitment to do the right thing. The Holy Spirit is ever present. May he anoint our days and decisions so that we might be one with him.

Lord, let your love flow through me in the Holy Spirit.

FEBRUARY 17

Rejoice in hope, endure in affliction, persevere in prayer.
Romans 12:12

One of the best things we can do before we even get out of bed in the morning is to rejoice. When we rejoice, we don't necessarily have to feel happy. We might even feel scared or sad. But no matter how we feel, we are free to offer our gratitude, adoration, and commitment to God because he is all-good and deserving of it. Rejoicing in hope means to revel in awe and wonder at the almighty power and presence of God. Rejoice! It's good for the soul.

Lord, I rejoice in the wonder of you.

FEBRUARY 18

Do not let me be put to shame,
for I have called to you, Lord.
Psalm 31:18

The enemy of our souls uses shame to trap us in the darkness of our fears. Shame keeps us cowering in the corner of our lives, hoping the enemy won't expose us as the awful, unlovable, or unacceptable people he tells us we are.

Every overblown and false fear we experience is fueled by shame. It robs us of our ability to experience authentic joy and freedom in Christ. There is a great deal that we can do psychologically to heal from shame, but only Jesus can set us free completely. Shame is a spiritual stronghold that must be broken.

Lord, break my shame.

FEBRUARY 19

"Lazarus, come out!"
John 11:43

Many people have used the story of Lazarus as a guide for healing from the wounds of shame. Lazarus had been in the tomb for four days when Jesus raised him from the dead. There would have been a stench. Nevertheless, Jesus commanded Lazarus to come out.

Why didn't Jesus go into the cave to get him? Scripture doesn't say, but that detail is a source of meditation for those who deal with shame. Shame is long lasting and causes a stench in our spirit. But Jesus calls us, as he called Lazarus, and we must make the choice to leave the old, putrid burial cloths behind. We must walk out of the darkness and shadows of our shame into Christ's loving light. There he will reveal the beautiful truth of who we are for all to see.

Lord, send me the courage to step out of my shame.

FEBRUARY 20

Lord, I love the refuge of your house,
the site of the dwelling-place of your glory.
Psalm 26:8

We are blessed to be able to enter the Lord's house any time we choose. We are all welcome in the dwelling place of the Lord. We often hear it said that the church is not a museum for saints, but a hospital for sinners. Jesus calls us, saying, "Those who are well do not need a physician, but the sick do. I did not come to call the righteous but sinners" (Mark 2:17). The Holy Mass is the greatest source of healing we have this side of heaven, but we can also find healing and comfort when we stop in at church where Jesus is present in the Tabernacle. He waits patiently for us to pay him a visit so that we can be well.

Lord, I am grateful that you are near.

FEBRUARY 21

"For God all things are possible."
Matthew 19:26

The trouble with fear is that it narrows our view. The more anxious we are, the less open we are to inspiration and the less able to examine alternatives in a situation. When this closing in begins to happen, it is good to pry open the door to possibility by remembering and repeating the verse for today's reflection: "For God all things are possible."

The first step to solving any problem is acknowledging that we don't have all the answers. In doing so, we are better able to remain open and curious about the infinite possibilities that await us in God's good solutions for our lives. Look up and let God in.

Lord, help me to remain open and curious.

FEBRUARY 22

When cares increase within me,
your comfort give me joy.
Psalm 94:19

There is a natural rhythm to the life of our souls. We alternate between times of consolation and desolation. Both seasons are important for our well-being and growth.

In consolation we experience a deep abiding sense of God's presence, and we are stirred to seek greater union with him.

St. Ignatius of Loyola defines desolation as "darkness of the soul, turmoil of the mind, . . . restlessness resulting from many disturbances and temptations . . . , when a soul finds itself completely apathetic, tepid, sad, and separated . . . from its Creator and Lord."[8] God allows desolation as a means to strengthen our spiritual resolve—it keeps us humble and close to his heart.

In desolation, we are pressed into battle to increase the intensity of our prayers, regardless of how we feel, and to rely on more frequent reception of the Eucharist. We offer up our sufferings for that which will bring greater good in our world. Your times of desolation are a grace from God.

Lord, purify my heart.

FEBRUARY 23

Consider it all joy, my brothers, when you encounter various trials, for you know that the testing of your faith produces perseverance.
James 1:2-3

You may be struggling, but that does not mean you are failing. A little child makes many attempts before finally taking that first step; a butterfly beats its wings against the confines of the chrysalis for days before emerging in its fullness; Jesus fell three times along the road to the greatest victory of all.

Instead of beating ourselves up because we struggle, we should learn to embrace our struggles as a means to a better end. This is key to finding peace in our days. Struggle has its own value. It is necessary for our growth and well-being. Do not be surprised when you are tested beyond your limits, for God means to expand your territory. Let him.

Lord, bring it on. I'm ready.

FEBRUARY 24

"I have told you this so that my joy may be in you and your joy may be complete."
John 15:11

What an amazing gift—Jesus shares his joy with us! We cannot fathom what his joy must be like in its fullness because what we experience here is a tiny glimpse of the heavenly joy that awaits us. But the fact that Jesus wants to complete our joy is awesome and wonderful! When he spoke these words about joy in today's verse, Jesus had just finished talking about his relationship with his Father, offering his followers the parable of the vine and the branches and telling them to keep his commands.

This is important. Obedience matters. When we follow God's rules and God's ways, we can't help but be on the perfect path to pure and complete joy. One step at a time, we'll get there.

Lord, set me on the path to joy.

FEBRUARY 25

All scripture is inspired by God and is useful for teaching,
for refutation, for correction, and for
training in righteousness.
2 Timothy 3:16

We can't force people to think as we do or believe what we believe. As much as we would like consensus, or agreement, or even a small measure of understanding, these can be difficult to achieve.

We want people to know what we know about the things of God, but ultimately it is the Holy Spirit who stirs their hearts and enlightens their minds toward God. The best thing we can do is pray for an opening, a crack in their armor; we can pray that they will have a teachable and reachable heart. Our first pope also gave us the following good advice:

But in your hearts revere Christ as Lord.
Always be prepared to give an answer
to everyone who asks you to give the reason for
the hope that you have.
But do this with gentleness and respect. (1 Peter 3:15, NIV)

Holy Spirit, give me the words.

FEBRUARY 26

Those who gain sense truly love themselves;
those who preserve understanding will find success.
Proverbs 19:8

Our best is always good enough. When we affirm today's best, we make way for a better tomorrow. Berating ourselves because we think that we should do more than we are capable of or be more than we are is neither fair nor just. Never being satisfied with ourselves or our progress is a trap. The goal is not to be perfect, but to be the best that we can be today. We find greater energy to pursue excellence when we accept who we are and where we are at this point in our lives. We should do so lovingly and with great compassion for what we have been through.

If we mess up today, we get another chance tomorrow. Today's best is still something to celebrate.

Lord, today you have my best.

FEBRUARY 27

*"You loved justice and hated wickedness;
therefore God, your God, anointed you
with the oil of gladness."*
Hebrews 1:9

J oy and holiness go hand in hand; you can't have true joy
without holiness, and you can't have holiness without joy.
Holiness isn't boring and devoid of the good things in life.
Nothing could be further from the truth. Daily pursuit of holiness brings fulfillment, depth, meaning, and purpose. Holiness, by definition, means to be set aside for God. When we consecrate ourselves to God, an unfolding of grace brings everything into proper perspective, and we know joy from the inside out.

Lord, I seek holiness and joy.

FEBRUARY 28

"Until now you have not asked anything in my name; ask and you will receive, so that your joy may be complete."
John 16:24

God delights in answering our prayers. He wants to fulfill our every desire, but he can't and won't unless we ask. Even then, he will only give us what is in our best interest because that is the only way we can be filled with joy. God is love, and he will only do the most loving thing.

When we pray in Jesus' name, he is an active messenger, presenting our petitions, needs, and desires before the throne of God. He helps us, through the Holy Spirit, to seek and know the Father's will. Prayer is a dynamic dialogue that engages the entire Holy Trinity in a conversation of the heart, so that we can truly know joy.

Jesus, Holy Spirit, and almighty God my Father, hear and answer me.

MARCH

MARCH 1

"Blessed are the peacemakers,
for they will be called children of God."
Matthew 5:9

The whole world is longing for peace, and so is every human heart. God knows this, and maybe that's why peace is mentioned over four hundred times in Scripture: peace is on God's heart too. Peace is a worthy pursuit and a promise from God. He delivers the gift of his peace in all sorts of packages. Sometimes it comes wrapped in struggle; other times we enjoy the beauty of his consolation. Yet peace is an ever-present possibility.

Claim God's peace today. As his child, it is part of your inheritance.

Lord, bring your peace.

MARCH 2

*"Come to me, all you who labor and are burdened, and I
will give you rest. "*
Matthew 11:28

We often need to take a step back to get ahead. There is
no failure in having to regroup, let go, or take a break.
When the clamoring crowd surrounded them, Jesus invited
his disciples to "come away by [themselves] to a deserted place
and rest a while" (Mark 6:31).

That sound's wonderful, doesn't it? Jesus is forever asking us
to come to him. It's an open and ongoing invitation to enter
more deeply into a relationship with him. He is beckoning
us to join him on a better path where our busy lives are transformed and where he carries our burdens.

Lord, I accept your invitation.

MARCH 3

Let us love not in word or speech but in deed and truth.
I John 3:18

God multiplies his love in our hearts when we share it. We can never run out! God's love will lead us to affirm the dignity and worth of others, desire their highest good, and offer them mercy and forgiveness when they fail us.

Our acts of service, works of mercy, and tiny sacrifices for others do not go unnoticed by God, and they are especially blessed when we offer them in a hidden, heartfelt manner. Further, loving others helps us to be more loving toward ourselves. Jesus tells us that when we lose our lives for others, we save our own (see Luke 17:33). One way to do this is to offer a loving act of service without expecting anything in return.

Holy Spirit, reveal an opportunity in which I can love someone today.

MARCH 4

Nothing gives me greater joy than to hear that my children
are walking in the truth.
3 John 1:4

It's one thing to acknowledge our pain and another thing to wallow in it. When we shape our identity around the way we are hurting, we are not walking in the whole truth of who we are called to be. There is a time, as we are recovering, when we need to identify ourselves as a victim and give voice to the way we have been hurt, but we cannot stay there. At some point, we need to stop counting the cost and move on. We can trust the next step in our healing, whatever that may be. But it will not come until we are ready to let go and walk in the truth that God will heal our hurts when we let him.

Lord, heal me.

MARCH 5

Let the peace of Christ control your hearts, the peace into which you were also called in one body.
Colossians 3:15

We find peace, not in the absence of conflict, but in our ability to deal with conflict. Storms serve a purpose in our lives. They teach us, they strengthen us, and they reveal the truth of God's fidelity and sustaining love for us. They may be intense, they may be unpredictable, but they never last. And it is possible to remain peaceful in their midst.

Conflict too, whether it is with someone else or within ourselves, may be necessary in order to get to the other side of a problem or improve a relationship. When we start to think of our problems as opportunities for growth, we will buoy ourselves with a brighter outlook.

Lord, teach me how to weather the storms.

MARCH 6

"Do this in memory of me."
Luke 22:19

The Mass is a love letter from God. He writes it on our hearts so that we'll never, ever forget how much he loves us. At the first Mass, the Last Supper, Jesus poured his heart out and offered himself as a holy and living sacrifice for us. He freely chose to do this: true love can only be given in freedom.

The graces we receive at Mass help us to love more freely and rid ourselves of the compulsions and impure motivations that drive us. It's not a bad thing to love out of obligation, but God wants something more for us. He is forever calling us to a deeper, freer love. We share that love with others in memory of him.

Lord, free my heart.

MARCH 7

"He must increase; I must decrease."
John 3:30

As we go through life, we accumulate attitudes and interior dispositions that may no longer be useful. We might assume that we have no choice regarding how we react to circumstances, especially difficult ones. Lent reminds us that we can cast off the old ways and welcome new choices and a whole new way of thinking about the world.

Allowing ourselves to be purged can be a painful process. We have to let go of some things we hold dear, such as ways of behaving that, while comfortable and familiar, may need to decrease for our own good. The season of Lent is a good time for reflecting on these behaviors as we prepare for the resurrection of better things to come.

Holy Spirit, reveal what must decrease in me.

MARCH 8

"Do whatever he tells you."
John 2:5

Pope St. John Paul II often used the beautiful word *entrustment* when he talked about Mary. He entrusted his entire pontificate and his very life to her through total consecration to Jesus through her. His motto was *Totus tuus*—"totally yours." Maybe you hesitate to entrust everything to Mary because you think it will detract from your relationship with Jesus. But Mary would never lead us away from her Son. St. Maximillian Kobe reminds us that we can never love Mary more than Jesus does.

Mary's entire purpose is to point us toward Jesus. From the moment of his conception to the first miracle at Cana until this present moment, she has been encouraging us to draw near to Jesus and do whatever he tells us. What we entrust to Mary finds its way directly to the center of Jesus' heart, through her own loving and immaculate heart.

Mary, help me to trust more and more.

MARCH 9

When you pass through waters, I will be with you;
through rivers, you shall not be swept away.
Isaiah 43:2

I stood in the dimly lit hospital corridor at midnight, struggling to listen to the doctor as I watched a team of nurses
swiftly maneuver the gurney that carried my husband down
to ICU. "Your husband has had a stroke, and there is nothing we can do . . ." The nurse said more, but I didn't catch it,
and then I was standing there, in the middle of my suddenly
changed life—alone. As the tsunami of terror welled up inside
me, I remembered that I had two choices: I could either let
it overtake me, or I could trust.

The choice to trust gave way to a merciful numbing—I could
almost see Jesus stretching out his hand of grace to keep me
from going under. Those are the moments in life that you
think you will never survive—but you do, and you realize how
truly small you are and how big his love can be.

Lord, carry me.

MARCH 10

Attend to yourself and to your teaching; persevere in both tasks, for by doing so you will save both yourself and those who listen to you.

1 Timothy 4:16

Healthy boundaries are essential for self-care. From time to time, it's good to check in with yourself to determine if you are leaving encounters with others feeling drained, resentful, misunderstood, or violated. These feelings can linger, and they indicate that you have weak or nonexistent boundaries. You may have relinquished to someone else your own responsibility to make yourself feel better.

If you are waiting for another person to change so that you can feel good, safe, peaceful, or well, then you need to do some boundary work. The first step is self-awareness.

Take time to pray and reflect on what you want, need, and feel. You could list those wants, needs, and feelings in three columns and then fill them in with your thoughts. Look for patterns, and pay attention to how you feel as you do this.

Holy Spirit, enlighten me.

MARCH 11

For you have snatched me from death,
kept my feet from stumbling,
That I may walk before God
in the light of the living.
Psalm 56:14

We can step outside of "the light of the living" in many ways. To cope with stress, we might take up a mind-numbing activity as a distraction, only to find out that it has a greater hold on us than we would like. If you have been stumbling in the dark, today you can come into the light.

What activity brings you to life, engaging all of your senses? Is it painting, or running, or decorating your home? Cooking, or gardening, or going to a sporting event? Remember, you have five senses: touch, taste, sight, hearing, and smell.

To walk in the light of the living means to live in the fullness of God. There, fears and worries take a back seat to the delights he wants to share with you today.

Lord, lead me to your light.

MARCH 12

"Be still, and know that I am God!"
Psalm 46:10 (NIV)

Those times when I have managed to depend completely on God, he has never let me down. I may not have received exactly what I wanted, nor have I always been spared from suffering. Yet when I was able to totally surrender and let God be God, I experienced some of the best moments of my life.

Most of the time, we aren't even aware of how much we wrestle with God for control. He tries to get our attention, but we stay stuck in self-sufficiency mode. When was the last time you radically trusted God to take over in a difficult situation?

Lord, help me to be still.

MARCH 13

For in this hope we were saved. But hope that is seen is no hope at all. Who hopes for what they already have? But if we hope for what we do not yet have, we wait for it patiently.
Romans 8:24-25 (NIV)

How can people go through unspeakable tragedies or soul-shattering disappointments and still say, with all sincerity, "I'm blessed"? It's because of the miracle and mystery of hope.

The *Modern Catholic Dictionary* defines *hope* as "the confident desire of obtaining a future good that is difficult to attain."[9] Hope is not positive or wishful thinking; it's a condition of the heart that holds firm to the conviction that good will come in the future with no proof of it in the present.

Hope is infused in our souls in Baptism. We spend the rest of our lives being strengthened in and by hope.

Lord, fill me with hope.

MARCH 14

For they preferred human praise to the glory of God.
John 12:43

PeOple pleasing is exhausting, but it can be disingenuous too. Think about it: telling people what they want to hear means that you will have to become like a chameleon, changing your mind to appeal to every taste and circumstance. We lose ourselves when we do that. We want to be nice, and we don't want to make waves, but people pleasing is actually a symptom of human pride.

In fact, Jesus said this: "How terrible it will be for you when everyone says nice things about you, because that's the way their ancestors used to treat the false prophets" (Luke 6:26, ISV). Yikes! Let's please God instead.

Lord, I only want to please you.

MARCH 15

Jesus Christ is the same yesterday, today, and forever.
Hebrews 13:8

Some days are better than others. We experience days when it's easy to cope, while other days it's nearly impossible to get out of bed in the morning. Some days it feels like we are walking on air, and on others we're bored to tears. The one thing that is constant about being human is that we're always changing.

Remember two things. First, this too shall pass. Nothing stays constant, and breakthroughs happen every day. Second, Jesus is unchanging. We can count on him to be there as a firm foundation. He's not fickle or arbitrary. He is, and he always will be. On that we can depend.

These two points can help us stay focused and weather the ups and downs of life.

Lord, thank you for being the same yesterday,
today, and always.

MARCH 16

He is not the God of disorder but of peace.
1 Corinthians 14:33

How comfortable are you with peace and tranquility? For some of us, fearfulness is such a constant state of being that it feels normal. The absence of anxiety can be so foreign to our experience that peace seems uncomfortable or boring. We end up feeling guilty when we don't have something to worry about.

So how do we get comfortable with peace? We invite the Holy Spirit into our worries. In prayer, ask him to show you patterns or habits that indicate you are clinging to problems, situations, people, or fears. We often do this because we don't believe we deserve to be at peace or because we don't know how to accept serenity. Whatever the root cause of worry, the Lord has a plan to get you to the promised land of peace. Follow him.

Holy Spirit, show me how I may be resisting your peace.

MARCH 17

Behind and before you encircle me
and rest your hand upon me.
Psalm 139:5

In celebration of St. Patrick's feast day, here is an excerpt from a prayer known as St. Patrick's Breastplate. It's a good prayer for those of us with anxiety, reminding us that we're never alone.

Christ with me,
Christ before me,
Christ behind me,
Christ in me,
Christ beneath me,
Christ above me,
Christ on my right,
Christ on my left,
Christ when I lie down,
Christ when I sit down,
Christ when I arise,
Christ in every eye that sees me,
Christ in every ear that hears me.[10]

Amen.

MARCH 18

"Can any of you by worrying add a single moment to your life-span?"
Matthew 6:27

Perpetual worry can be a form of control, but it's an illusion. We can't manipulate anything with our worries. We can't influence the outcome of events, or make God or others do what we want by worrying. When you put most of your precious energy into worrying, you have less of it to solve problems, or pray, or embrace the peace that God wants to give you.

Lord, deliver me from worry.

MARCH 19

SOLEMNITY OF ST. JOSEPH

Joseph her husband [was] a righteous man.

Matthew 1:19

The Bible calls St. Joseph a "righteous man"—Jesus was obedient to him as well as to Mary (see Luke 2:51). Many people pray to St. Joseph for the protection of their families, for help with employment, or even to sell their homes. St. Joseph is said to be present at the time of death for those who call on him.

We can entrust our cares to him. St. Teresa of Avila said of St. Joseph "I have never known anyone who was truly devoted to him and honored him . . . who did not advance greatly in virtue: for he helps in a special way those souls who commend themselves to him."[11]

God entrusted his Son to St. Joseph. We can be assured that in him we have a steadfast friend and support.

Thank you, Father, for our spiritual provider and protector, St. Joseph.

MARCH 20

"And if he wrongs you seven times in one day and returns
to you seven times saying, 'I am sorry,' you
should forgive him."
Luke 17:4

Forgiveness unlocks the door to inner peace. Remember this: the Lord doesn't require more from us than we can give. He would never set us up for failure like that. Jesus commands us to forgive because he is prepared to give us the grace to do it. The question is whether we will receive or reject that grace.

There is nothing easy about forgiveness. We can't do it on our own. It's a gradual unfolding until the sting leaves our souls, and we are set free from carrying the heavy weight of our woundedness.

Every act of forgiveness is an act of freedom that only we can choose in our specific situations.

Lord, send your grace.

MARCH 21

Be transformed by the renewal of your mind.
Romans 12:2

Dread is the opposite of peace. It's a feeling that grips our hearts and invades our minds. It paralyzes us or propels us to take cover when we face a difficulty.

We can change our "dread response" into a habitual one of expecting good. It takes practice, but we can rewire our thoughts so that situations or people that used to stir up dread can stimulate an expectancy of a greater good. The first step is to move the needle of our dread response to a neutral position.

When we are neutral, we do not automatically define a situation as good or bad. Instead, we accept it as it is, viewing it objectively instead of emotionally. We're all capable of this, but we need to work at it. Ask the Holy Spirit to help you.

Come, Holy Spirit, transform my mind.

MARCH 22

Cast all your worries upon him because he cares for you.
1 Peter 5:7

The God of the universe cares for us; he's concerned about our well-being. He counts every hair on our heads, collects our tears, and lovingly tends to every little detail of our lives. It could be no other way for a God who *is* love. So why doesn't he take away our fears and anxieties? If he loves us, why do we have to suffer through so much doubt and worry? Maybe so that we will seek his peace that much more. Jesus tells us that his peace is not of this world—it's much better.

Let's not settle for anything less than what God wants to give us. He will care for us and calm our fears right now.

Lord, fill me with your peace.

MARCH 23

*We know that all things work
for good for those who love God.*
Romans 8:28

Many of the saints had to contend with excessive worry, trials, and tribulations. Their example should inspire us, assuring us that God can use even our worries to bring about heroic virtue and spiritual strength. Dealing with our daily stress and strife is one way that we take up our cross and follow Jesus to our heavenly home.

St. Paul of the Cross offers some advice:

When you notice that your heart is moving away even the tiniest bit from that inner peace that comes from the living faith-experience of the divine presence in the soul, stop and examine what the cause of this anxiety might be. Maybe it is some worry concerning your house or children, or some situation you cannot change at present. Bury it in God's loving will.[12]

Sounds like a plan!

Lord, I bury my anxieties in your loving will.

MARCH 24

*Do not fear: I am with you; / do not be anxious: I am your
God. / I will strengthen you, I will help you, / I will uphold
you with my victorious right hand.*

Isaiah 41:10

Most people are familiar with the short version of the
Serenity Prayer: "God grant me the serenity to accept
the things I cannot change; courage to change the things I
can; and wisdom to know the difference."[13] As a prescription
for life, this prayer has it all.

First, we turn to God as the source of our peace because
there is no peace on earth that compares to his. Then, acceptance of our limitations becomes the first step toward freedom.
Courage to change flows from a confidence that is rooted in
a right relationship with God. We acknowledge his loving will
and focus our efforts on changing the only thing that we can:
ourselves.

Finally, the beautiful gift of wisdom from the Holy Spirit
grows through obedience. It also helps us to lead correctly-
ordered lives that will not be disturbed by every pressing storm.

God, grant me your goodness.

MARCH 25

For lack of guidance a people falls;
security lies in many counselors.
Proverbs 11:14

When the devil tempted Jesus in the desert, he offered him quick fixes. But when the angel comforted Jesus in his agony in the garden, he did not take away his suffering. Instead, the angel came alongside him and ministered to him, offering comfort and consolation. This image of Jesus in the garden with the angel by his side reminds us that none of us, not even Jesus, can avoid suffering, but we have many means, both heavenly and earthly, to find comfort.

Jesus didn't go into the garden alone. He brought friends along, and even though they let him down by falling asleep, he repeatedly went to them for help. The truth is, we need each other, not just during life-and-death situations, but for the daily trials of life. Don't be afraid to reach out. If your friends disappoint you, keep looking for support. There are no quick fixes, but there will always be someone in heaven or on earth who will walk with you on the way toward peace.

Lord, send me an angel.

MARCH 26

Have no anxiety at all, but in everything, by prayer and petition, with thanksgiving, make your requests known to God.
Philippians 4:6

Thanksgiving and gratitude are powerful elixirs for the anxious heart. It is nearly impossible to feel fear and gratitude at the same time. Gratitude expands the heart, and fear constricts it. When we start to recount all that we are thankful for, a shift takes place in our minds. Our thoughts focus on how much we are filled, not on what we lack. When we pray, and ask, and thank, our hearts and minds are engaged in worthwhile, life-giving pursuits. These actions lead to a special kind of peace.

Lord, I am deeply grateful for _____.

MARCH 27

Then the peace of God that surpasses all understanding will guard your hearts and minds in Christ Jesus.
Philippians 4:7

We know what happens when negativity and fear take over, but God intends that we walk in his heavenly peace. He has given us the way, through Jesus, to receive that peace.

We need to guard our spirits, keeping watch over what we allow to infiltrate our thoughts and invade our hearts. These are precious territories that require preservation and cultivation. Peace will protect us, but we can't let the enemy in through the back door of negativity and fear.

Lord, be my guard.

MARCH 28

Though the mountains fall away
and the hills be shaken,
My love shall never fall away from you
nor my covenant of peace be shaken,
says the LORD, who has mercy on you.
Isaiah 54:10

Anytime we seek God, he's eager to reveal himself to us. This might be through Scripture or in prayer or when we receive him in the Eucharist. Through the words of the prophets, God is quick to remind us that we have an unbreakable covenant of love with him. In the passage for today, he also reminds us of his promise of peace.

Our world is not always going to be peaceful on the outside, but we can experience an unshakable peace on the inside. Today let us believe that we have received that peace. Peace is a gift that God is giving all the time. You will have it when you need it. Just believe.

Lord, I believe in your covenant of peace with me.

MARCH 29

In all these things we conquer overwhelmingly through him who loved us.

Romans 8:37

We are not destined to be depressed, overwhelmed, defeated, or ashamed. We are created for victory in Christ. As with any battle, we rarely win overnight. We're equipped to be overcomers, but we will only overcome through our own hard work and a daily (sometimes hourly) commitment to get to the other side of our inner mountains.

There are many weapons at our disposal. Prayer, the Rosary, counseling, medication, hospitalization, spiritual direction, exercise, friendships, the sacraments, Eucharistic Adoration, or a combination of the above. Daily maneuvers might include accepting grace, faking it till you make it, total surrender, asking for help, or pushing through.

A victory can be anything from finding the energy to tackle the dishes in the sink to having the courage to face some of the darkest places in your soul. God gives us the grace to keep pressing on toward the finish line.

Lord, help me press on to victory.

MARCH 30

Each one should test their own actions. Then they can take pride in themselves alone, without comparing themselves to someone else.
Galatians 6:4 (NIV)

Claire took five steps toward freedom from comparing herself with others.

First, she replaced the defeating mental habit of comparison with a positive one of affirmation, such as, "I, Claire, am good enough in the eyes of God." Second, she prayed daily for a breakthrough that would help free her from the feeling that she never measured up. Third, she resisted negative influences and people who triggered the comparison habit in her or who fueled jealousies. Fourth, she set an achievable and specific goal to complete one new project without worrying about what anybody else said about it. Fifth, she took full responsibility for making these changes.

Try these steps to free yourself from any bad habit.

Lord, help me to kick the habit of comparing myself with others.

MARCH 31

*All of us . . . are being transformed into the
same image from glory to glory.*
2 Corinthians 3:18

When God made us, he made us in his image and declared
that we are good. Our behaviors and tendency toward
sin may bring us down and cause us pain, but it was never
God's intention for us to suffer or be separated from him.
Our first parents, Adam and Eve, changed that, but their sin
was not the end of the story. God went to plan B . . . the plan
of redemption through Jesus Christ. In him, we are baptized
into the way of grace and transformation in the Spirit of God.

Day by day, God sets us free from our sins and restores our
relationship with him. He is the almighty Change Agent, the
Makeover Specialist for our souls. He will never give up on
us, and neither should we.

Dear God, transform and restore my soul.

APRIL

APRIL 1

*With all humility and gentleness, with patience, bearing
with one another through love.*
Ephesians 4:2

Patience and humility are entwined in a virtuous duet. Patience is necessary if we are to grow in humility, and humility enables us to be truly patient with ourselves and others. As a prescription for living, the pursuit of these virtues will lead us to a deep sense of self-possession, anchored by grace.

Self-possession is another valuable trait. It empowers us to keep our composure under stress and tap into an inner strength that is not dependent on circumstances. It guards us against emotional overreaction, becoming overwhelmed, experiencing despair, and moodiness. Sounds wonderful, doesn't it?

*Lord, help me to grow in humility, patience, and
self-possession!*

APRIL 2

My flesh also shall rest in hope.
Psalm 16:9 (KJV)

At least once a day, you probably say, "I hope . . ." We hope for sunny weather, an end to a sickness, a good grade, or some other positive outcome. As Christians, we do indeed "rest in hope" for the coming of our Savior and the good things that God has promised us.

The *Catechism of the Catholic Church* says that hope

keeps man from discouragement; it sustains him during times of abandonment; it opens up his heart in expectation of eternal beatitude. Buoyed up by hope, he is preserved from selfishness and led to the happiness that flows from charity. (1818)

In other words, hope leads to love, and we need both to survive in this world. Let's remember to pray for an increase in hope.

Lord, infuse me with a holy hope.

APRIL 3

*We do not know how to pray as we ought, but the Spirit
itself intercedes with inexpressible groanings.*
Romans 8:26

When we enter into prayer, we not only pray through the
Holy Spirit—we also pray with Mary, the angels and
saints in heaven, and the souls in purgatory, in a language of
love that will be spoken for all eternity. Prayer is powerful and
unifying. Even when we don't know how to pray or have run
out of ways to pray, the Holy Spirit takes over on our behalf.

As a friend once told me, God knows exactly where our
prayers need to go. He receives them and then applies them
in order to bring about his perfect plan. With all of this heavenly help, we can rest assured that our prayers will be effective.

*Thank you, Holy Spirit, angels of God, and the communion
of saints, for your constant intercession.*

APRIL 4

For I know well the plans I have in mind for you—
*[declares] the L*ORD*—plans for your welfare and not for*
woe, so as to give you a future of hope.
Jeremiah 29:11

A woman developed a drinking problem in college that threatened her young life. She hit bottom when she was involved in a serious car accident. This got the attention of her family, who sent her to a Christian rehabilitation center. The treatment was successful.

The young woman not only got sober, but she also renewed her relationship with Jesus. Life was good, but she struggled to find her purpose and prayed for direction. Then one day, she picked up a paintbrush thinking that expressing herself through art might help calm her anxiety. She had found the answer to her prayers.

She discovered that her vibrant painting style was marketable. She identified her calling, and with it, the means to support herself. Today, as a successful artist, she uses her God-given talent to bring joy to others as she shares her witness of what Jesus has done in her life.

Lord, show me my purpose.

APRIL 5

Whoever heeds life-giving correction
will be at home among the wise.
Proverbs 15:31 (NIV)

"You think too much." "You're way too sensitive!" "Why don't you just relax?" How many times have you heard these comments? Sometimes they are meant to be helpful and other times dismissive, but we don't have to absorb any shame that might come from them. The truth is, we probably *do* spend too much time trying to figure things out in our heads, and we may be more touchy than we need to be, but these are part of our journey. This is who we are on the way to who we are becoming. If we need to make modifications or changes, we will make them. If we are called to embrace and celebrate our deep sensitivity, we can do that too.

There is a saying in Twelve Step circles: "Take what you want and leave the rest behind." It reminds us that we can sift through the messages we receive each day and determine what we should take to heart and what doesn't apply.

Lord, thank you for this journey.

APRIL 6

You do not possess because you do not ask.

James 4:2

What's on your heart today? What do you need? What do you want? God is not Santa Claus, but he is listening. He even plants those desires in your heart so that he can fulfill them. How he wants to fulfill them may be different from what you are expecting, but that doesn't mean that he hasn't heard you.

Have you let him know your need? Have you spoken it out loud in prayer? The Letter to the Hebrews invites us to go boldly to "God's throne of grace with confidence, so that we may receive mercy and find grace to help us in our time of need" (Hebrews 4:16, NIV). Let this inspire you today. Ask, so that you may receive.

Lord, I want _____.

APRIL 7

Seek what is above,
where Christ is seated at the right hand of God.
Think of what is above, not of what is on earth.
Colossians 3:1-2

Having a heavenly perspective changes everything. The things of this world are going to pass away for something far better—this is not our true home. If we can remember that, then we can see that those worries that loom large and ominous before us are really a small matter compared to all eternity. I always ask myself, "Is this going to matter in ten years or when I get to heaven?" Chances are I won't even remember the struggle or challenge three weeks from now!

Thinking about things that are above doesn't mean having our heads in the clouds. It means having our priorities straight and our attention and attachments properly focused.

Lord, I lift my eyes and heart toward you.

APRIL 8

Let the word of Christ dwell in you richly.
Colossians 3:16

In times of stress, the word of God is one of our best weapons in the battle against overload. We can claim it, we can apply it, and we can repeat it, until it sinks into our spirits. Scripture says that the Word of God is "living and effective, sharper than any two-edged sword" (Hebrews 4:12). Sometimes we need protection against the powers and principalities out there, and the weapon of the word of God is a powerful aid. When Jesus spoke the word of God, the devil cowered in the desert. When Peter spoke the word to the crowds on Pentecost, thousands were converted.

We can arm ourselves with Scripture verses that uplift, affirm, and quiet our souls, so that no matter what storm is swirling around us, we have an anchor in the word.

Your word, O Lord, is my strength and my shield.

APRIL 9

The LORD is my strength and my shield,
in whom my heart trusts,
I am helped, so my heart rejoices;
My heart leaps for joy,
with my song I praise him.
Psalm 28:7

We cannot underestimate the power of praising God. It increases everything good in our hearts, because our hearts were made for praise. Just ten minutes of praise in the morning, either through prayer or song or both, can set us on course to receive everything that day as a gift from God. Praise heals us and helps us to change from the inside out.

Praise is a daily workout for your soul. It pumps you up, it makes you stronger, and it's a good habit for a healthy heart!

Lord, I praise you.

APRIL 10

Just one thing: forgetting what lies behind but straining forward to what lies ahead, I continue my pursuit toward the goal, the prize of God's upward calling, in Christ Jesus.
Philippians 3:13-14

It's hard to let go of the past. We work through it, we wrestle with it, we reflect on it and rehash it, but the past is the past and there is nothing we can do about what happened. We can only influence what is yet to be. God purifies our past as we entrust our future to him. If he can use anything from the past to help us, he will use it. The rest he will cast away.

People often say that they'll forgive, but they won't forget. It's understandable. But just as some things are worth remembering, there are others that are best forgotten. Ask the Holy Spirit to show you how to let go of what's best forgotten.

Lord, I release my past to you.

APRIL 11

So let us confidently approach the throne of grace to receive mercy and to find grace for timely help.

Hebrews 4:16

Jesus, I trust in you. The soothing rays that flow from the heart of Jesus in the Divine Mercy image are a good focal point for prayer and reflection. They are referred to as the fountain of mercy, offering perpetual replenishment for wanting souls who feel far from God's love. Our worries and fears can place a wedge in our hearts, making us feel disconnected from God's care. The rays reach out and build a bridge to his loving heart.

When in doubt, simply repeat, *Jesus, I trust in you.* Let his cascading grace flow from his merciful heart to yours.

Jesus, I trust in you.

APRIL 12

May the God who gives endurance and encouragement give
you the same attitude of mind toward each other
that Christ Jesus had.
Romans 15:5 (NIV)

We can change and control our attitudes and subject them to our human will. Our attitudes are our responsibility, and our successes and failures depend largely on them. A good attitude will help get us where we want to go, and a bad attitude will ensure that we never get there.

As today's verse suggests, we need endurance and encouragement to maintain an attitude that reflects Christ. If you need a change of attitude, pray for it. Put out the heavenly help-wanted sign: Attitude Adjustment Needed.

Lord, help me change my attitude.

APRIL 13

The human heart plans the way,
but the LORD directs the steps.
Proverbs 16:9

One of the hardest things to do is to trust in God's timing when we want to accomplish something. As I waited through years of infertility to become a mother, I faced the possibility that my plans might not be God's plans. It was a great lesson in humility. As I struggled to accept the idea that biological motherhood would pass me by, my heart's cry was "Lord, please help me not to be bitter!"

When the Lord is establishing our steps, he is always doing it for our own good and the good of our souls. If we can trust in that and trust in him, we will experience a deep peace in knowing that all is as it should be, and all will be well in due time.

Lord, help me to trust in your plan.

APRIL 14

We have the mind of Christ.
1 Corinthians 2:16

There is hope for us because we have the mind of Christ. What do you think the mind of Christ is like? I think that it is completely serene, at one with the will of God, deeply engaged with thoughts that are full of faith, hope, love, joy, and service. Of this I'm certain: Christ's mind is not preoccupied with incriminating self-talk, concerns for the future, or regrets from the past. He is not plagued by intrusive thoughts or overrun with worries.

Ask Jesus to give you his mind even if, at the start, it is only a glimpse. As we grow in trust and surrender, more and more of our thoughts will become like his.

Lord, give me your mind!

APRIL 15

People look at the outward appearance, but the LORD looks at the heart.
1 Samuel 16:7 (NIV)

We are very good at putting our false selves out there for everybody to see. We wear masks of competence and control, fearing that if people knew the real person inside, they would not like us. But oh, how precious we are in God's sight—just the way we are. We may not always do the right thing, but God is mostly concerned with the condition of our hearts. According to Scripture, he is in the business of transforming and saving us as he observes and considers the health of our hearts.

What part of your heart needs repair? Ask the almighty physician and king of hearts to tend to what ails you.

Lord, heal my heart.

APRIL 16

Because you have the LORD for your refuge
and have made the Most High your stronghold,
No evil shall befall you.
Psalm 91:9-10

St. Benedict Joseph Labre, whose feast we celebrate today, is the pilgrim saint and patron of those who are homeless or mentally ill. After several religious orders rejected him, Benedict took up the life of a beggar. From his native France, he left on a pilgrimage to shrines in Rome and lived off alms for most of his life.

Benedict loved visiting Jesus in the Blessed Sacrament and often slept in churches or on their doorsteps. Even though he was poor, possessing nothing, he was known for his kindness and generosity. At the announcement of his death, the children in the neighborhood shouted in the streets, "The saint is dead."

Despite his own mental angst, St. Benedict found his home in Jesus. We can ask for him to intercede for us so that we can do the same.

St. Benedict Joseph, help me to make a home in God's heart.

APRIL 17

Love is patient, love is kind.
1 Corinthians 13:4

Patience with yourself is paramount. Treating yourself with gentleness and compassion is a necessary step in overcoming anxiety. The way you relate to yourself has an impact on all your relationships. You're worth the time and effort it takes to learn how to be patient and kind toward yourself.

There is another serenity prayer that works well toward this end. It is as follows:

God grant me the serenity
To stop beating myself up for not doing things perfectly,
The courage to forgive myself because I am working on doing better,
And the wisdom to know that you already love me just the way I am.[14]

Mastering the art of patience starts with ourselves.

Lord, let patience begin with me.

APRIL 18

Whoever is patient has great understanding.
Proverbs 14:29 (NIV)

St. Francis de Sales said it this way: "Have patience with all things, but chiefly have patience with yourself. Do not lose courage in considering your own imperfections but instantly set about remedying them—every day begin the task anew."[15]

We shouldn't be dismayed that we must work on patience every day. If we are growing, learning, and living life to the fullest, then we will also be starting over, stumbling, and seeking better and higher ways. Making mistakes and falling down are both part of the process of growing up in the spiritual life.

Take courage and carry on.

Lord, give me the strength to begin again.

APRIL 19

*Be still before the L*ORD*;*
wait for him.
Do not be provoked by the prosperous,
nor by malicious schemers.

Psalm 37:7

So many of our worries are tangled up in the actions of others. We experience stress when people treat us poorly, and we feel the need to speak up and defend ourselves. Naturally, we want to set the record straight. Yet when Jesus was accused wrongly, he said nothing. Today's verse suggests that we might do well to allow the Lord to defend us. We can wait and trust in him for the truth to come out.

This is difficult, but every time I have received the grace to do it, the situation has turned out well. Sometimes preserving the peace is a good idea, provided the situation is not abusive or in other ways harmful.

Lord, help me to be still.

APRIL 20

Let us not grow tired of doing good, for in due time we shall reap our harvest, if we do not give up.
Galatians 6:9

We might be tempted to think that we can't possibly become a saint because saints are known for their heroic virtue. But let's break it down. To be heroic is to keep trying against all odds. Heroes aren't always successful, but they never give up attempting to be. Remember—every saint was a sinner! Virtues are like seeds that God plants in our hearts. We nourish their growth in our lives as we participate in Mass, pray, and attend to our daily duties out of love for the Lord. Day by day, as we become rooted in his will, we grow in holiness. We may not be able to see it in ourselves, but it's there, and that's good.

Each one of us can cultivate heroic virtue, and we can all become saints because we can decide to keep trying, no matter what. We do our best, and God does the rest as we become all that he calls us to be.

Lord, make me a saint!

APRIL 21

For this is love, that we walk according to his commandments; this is the commandment, as you heard from the beginning, in which you should walk.

2 John 1:6

Parents feel loved and respected when their children follow their rules and listen to their instructions. God is no different. His commands to do or not do something flow from his love for us. He is not on a power trip. He is not trying to make our lives miserable. There is nothing in God that needs our obedience—and in fact, we are entirely free to disobey him. When we do, however, we are taking a step away from love instead of toward it.

People are often confused about what love is and how to give and receive it. Many equate love with indulgence and end up condoning damaging behavior. But if we make the connection between God's loving commands and our own good, we can begin to see that obeying his commands leads to peace and joy.

Lord, help me to obey.

APRIL 22

"The breath of the Almighty keeps me alive."
Job 33:4

*J*ust breathe. These are the words I text to my daughter when I know she is struggling with anxiety. They're the words I whisper to myself when I'm having a bad day. When you are having a similar kind of day, imagine the Holy Spirit filling you up as you draw in a long, deep breath of renewal and strength. The Holy Spirit is the breath of life. He brings clarity and a sense of rootedness in light and truth.

It doesn't take long to breathe in this manner, but it is highly effective. We don't need any system or well-developed practice to simply stop what we're doing and take a deep breath. These Holy Spirit-infused moments will sustain us and bring new life to our souls.

Holy Spirit, breathe in me.

APRIL 23

"Do not worry about tomorrow; tomorrow will take care of itself. Sufficient for a day is its own evil."
Matthew 6:34

Learning how to live in the present moment is an essential skill for the worriers of the world. Jesus taught about this more than once during his public ministry, and he seemed to follow his own advice when it came to living moment-to-moment. For most of us, it doesn't come naturally. But in faith, everything is possible with God in each present moment.

Spiritual writer Jean Pierre de Caussade, SJ, wrote: "The present moment is always filled with infinite treasure. It contains more than you have the capacity to hold."[16] When we release the past for the mysterious beauty and potential of what is in front of us right now, we will find God's "infinite treasure."

Lord, teach me to stay present to the eternal now.

APRIL 23

I have been crucified with Christ; yet I live, no longer I, but
Christ lives in me.
Galatians 2:19-20

It is so hard to let go of the need to control things and people, but this is how we die to ourselves daily so that Christ can live in us. If we have been hurt by something when we were powerless to do anything about it, it is natural to want to be in control. Being in control was a necessary coping mechanism that helped us handle the hurt. It may have served us in the past, but it's now getting in the way of our relationships with God, ourselves, and others.

We need to crucify the controlling spirit that plagues us because an excessive need to control doesn't relieve our anxiety—it increases it.

Lord, help me to let go.

APRIL 24

But do not ignore this one fact, beloved, that with the Lord one day is like a thousand years and a thousand years like one day.

2 Peter 3:8

Jill has had to work hard at time management. Her natural instinct is to put off until tomorrow what she ought to do today. She laments that she is never on time. Sometimes she apologizes and says, "I'm sorry . . . I'm on God's time!"

It does seem that God is never in a hurry, doesn't it? We have our timelines, deadlines, and prayers that we want answered yesterday, but God seems to take his time when it comes to revealing his will or answering certain prayers. Since God is the creator of time, I suppose he can do whatever he wants with it!

I have a plaque on my wall that says, "Everything happens at the time God chooses." That's another way of saying, "God's got this." Even when I don't think so, God is always on time.

Lord, I surrender my times to you.

APRIL 25

Pray without ceasing.
1 Thessalonians 5:17

I know a woman who prayed every day for over forty years for her son to give up drugs. There were many close calls and sleepless nights. She, her husband, and the entire family, including the son, went through unimaginable pain and a roller-coaster existence fraught with chaos and uncertainty.

Then one day, he quit. But the mother didn't stop praying. For the rest of her life, she offered prayers of thanksgiving, and she died with her son by her side. Wouldn't it be something if the Lord recorded all our prayers in a book for us to review with him when we get to heaven? All our prayers of petition, intercession, thanksgiving, praise, lament, and sorrow have been written on his heart. I want my book to be filled to overflowing, don't you?

Lord, hear our prayer.

APRIL 26

The LORD is with me; I am not afraid;
what can mortals do against me?
Psalm 118:6

Here's a thought: don't make friends with your fears. Don't invite them in, and don't feed them. When necessary, be prepared to kick them to the curb. If they somehow get in the back door, usher them out the front, and then lock them out for good.

Fears are like pesky neighbors—we don't have to entertain them. We can build a fence, observe them from a distance, and wave as they go by. We can appreciate fears for what they can tell us about certain situations and people, but they don't have to take up residence in our heads, because they always overstay their visit.

You are the keeper of your domain: mind, body, and spirit. You get to pick whom and what you let in. Choose your friends wisely.

Lord, help me to keep good company.

APRIL 27

For you do not desire sacrifice or I would give it;
a burnt offering you would not accept.
My sacrifice, O God, is a contrite spirit;
a contrite, humbled heart.
Psalm 51:18-19

If the Lord had to choose between your works and your heart, he would pick your heart every time. Good as our works might be, we can use them to keep God at a distance by becoming so busy that the clamor of our lives crowds him out. All relationships require time and attention. Our relationship with the Lord is no different.

He is waiting in every Tabernacle for hungry and humble hearts who seek him for his own sake. Is yours one of those hearts?

Lord, take my heart.

APRIL 28

"Amen, I say to you, unless you turn and become like children, you will not enter the kingdom of heaven."
Matthew 18:3

Depending on God is not a cop-out; it's a necessary disposition of the heart if we are to grow in spiritual maturity. In fact, the more childlike we become, the greater chance we have for holiness. Note: the goal is childlikeness, not childishness. There is a difference.

To change and become like children, we have to make some adult decisions. We need to decide to surrender our self-sufficiency in order to trust in God and his mercy. We need to make the decision to look for the goodness in others, forego guile, and give God permission to purify our hearts.

All of these decisions will lead to a place of great dependence, just where God calls us to be.

Lord, I am your child.

APRIL 29

I can do all things through Him who strengthens me.
Philippians 4:13 (NASB)

Today is the feast day of St. Catherine of Siena. She was a true spiritual spark plug who called out bishops and popes at a time when the Church was in turmoil. She loved God so intensely that she is said to have experienced a mystical marriage with Jesus. In her book, *Dialog of Catherine Siena,* she spoke of Jesus as a bridge by which we can safely cross over the raging waters of this life. God told her as recorded in the book that "I have given you the Bridge of My Son, in order that, passing across the flood, you may not be drowned, which flood is the tempestuous sea of this dark life."[17]

Our times are not that different from St. Catherine's. Her encouraging words can help us to always choose Jesus as we work our way through and over the sometimes turbulent waters of life.

St. Catherine, lead the way.

APRIL 30

In the morning you will hear my voice;
in the morning I will plead before you and wait.
Psalm 5:4

For most of my life, I woke up every morning gripped with fear and an overwhelming sense of dread for what the day would bring. Since I had experienced this as far back as I could remember, I didn't realize that there was any other way to be. As I gradually healed, and walked a journey of recovery with Jesus, I came to understand that this anxiety was *not* normal and that mornings could be peaceful and hopeful. Even joy was a possibility during those first moments of consciousness in the morning.

What a grace! Today's verse tells us to wait expectantly. I didn't do that because I didn't know I could expect anything different from what I had always experienced. Now I know that God wants to comfort, heal, and carry us through our days. Now you know it too! Expect it.

Lord, send me your peace and comfort from the moment of
my waking to the end of the day.

MAY

MAY 1

You will receive the unfading crown of glory.
1 Peter 5:4

When we crown a statue of Mary during the month of May, we symbolize her coronation as queen of heaven and earth and her virtuous perfection. We, her children, are also promised a crown. Scripture says,

> Blessed is the man who perseveres in temptation, for when he has been proved he will receive the crown of life that [God] promised to those who love him. (James 1:12)

Jesus also had his crown of thorns. St. Teresa of Calcutta said that it represented solidarity with those who struggle with depression, anxiety, or other mental illness. He wore his crown unto death so that we could obtain our crown of life. His crown of thorns becomes our crown of hope.

This month, search for the flowers among the thorns of your worries and anxieties. Ask Mary to fill you with the sweet fragrance of hope and joy.

Mary, I will walk with you.

MAY 2

Put on then, as God's chosen ones, holy and beloved,
heartfelt . . . kindness.
Colossians 3:12

Jackie refuses to make anyone an enemy, even those who try to make an enemy out of her. She's not doing this so that everyone will like her, but to interject the sorely needed virtue of kindness into the world.

Author Frank Viola describes the call to kindness as a "call to sacrifice, to embrace discomfort, to put action behind our words . . . , a way of life."[18] True kindness is motivated by love and demonstrated in authentically self-giving actions. It is not simply telling people what they want to hear or indulging them in their bad choices. True kindness empowers us to stand firm in our convictions while maintaining the dignity of others, especially those with whom we disagree.

Kindness has the potential to change the world. As a spiritual weapon and a fruit of the Holy Spirit, kindness can combat the simmering hostility and fear-driven actions that polarize us.

Lord, help me to be courageously and intentionally kind.

MAY 3

A clean heart create for me, God;
renew within me a steadfast spirit.
Psalm 51:12

"**L**ord, let me be motivated by love and not fear." This has been my daily prayer for most of my adult life. It is a cry of my heart because I know I can't do it on my own. Fear takes me into the realm of competition, comparison, and complete captivity to the lies that tell me I'm not good enough. Conversely, when I am motivated by love, I am free to be content, peaceful, and encouraging toward myself and others. Love is gentle and kind. In fear, I can become harsh, rigid, and unforgiving of myself and others.

The Lord can clean our hearts of all the fears that get in the way of love.

Lord, let it be so.

MAY 4

Because you are precious in my eyes
and honored, and I love you . . .
fear not for I am with you.
Isaiah 43:4, 5

We *do have a choice* to either listen to our fears or turn our attention to the love that flows straight from the heart of God. His love is communicated to us in Scripture time and time again. He says, for example, "With age-old love I have loved you" (Jeremiah 31:3). "I have called you by name: you are mine" (Isaiah 43:1).

When we focus on God's love, we are able to love ourselves the way God loves us. Not through self-indulgence or to satisfy our egos, but to embrace our dignity and value because of who God is. He is a loving and perfect Creator who doesn't make junk.

Lord, I embrace your love and let go of fear.

MAY 5

*If we acknowledge our sins, he is faithful and just and will
forgive our sins and cleanse us from every wrongdoing.*

1 John 1:9

Forgiving ourselves is an act of kindness. We do not have to
hold ourselves hostage to past mistakes or cling to excuses
that keep us from moving on. The Sacrament of Confession
can help us make a break with the past.

When we step into the confessional, we should keep in mind
the three conditions for making a good confession. First, we
need to state our sins simply, in kind and in number. We don't
have to elaborate, and we need only be as exact as we can be. If
the priest has questions for clarification, he will ask, but again,
the answers should be direct and simple. Second, we must be
contrite, meaning we are to be sorry for our sins. Third, we
must follow through on making amends or doing penance
as the priest prescribes. That is it. That is all. That is enough.

Lord, help me to forgive.

MAY 6

When I am afraid,
in you I place my trust.
Psalm 56:4

One way to put our trust in God is to pray a Rosary of trust. Whether we pray a decade or the entire Rosary, we dedicate each bead to a worry or difficulty we are experiencing. If we are worried about a meeting at work, for example, we ask for peace and presence of mind as we pray the Our Father or Hail Mary. If we are concerned about the welfare of a child, we ask Mary to wrap her mantle around that child, and so on.

The Rosary is an effective way to pray when we are anxious. St. Padre Pio called it a powerful weapon for our times. Use it wisely!

Mother Mary, guide me in trust.

MAY 7

There is an appointed time for everything,
and a time for every affair under the heavens.
Ecclesiastes 3:1

When fear was my primary motivation, silence was my enemy—I couldn't handle it. I filled my life with constant activity and compulsive pursuit of projects, fueled by a deep restlessness. I needed to fill up every waking minute to keep the fear at bay.

I understand now that God speaks in silence, and the enemy of my soul didn't want me to hear God. Through prayer, spiritual guidance, counseling, and living a sacramental life, God has replaced that fear with love. Today, life is manageable, balanced, and intentional. I can be still, wait, and soak in the silence. The tyranny of frenzied activity and noise is over.

Let this be your goal. It is possible!

Lord, settle me.

MAY 8

"If anyone wishes to be first, he shall be the last of all and the servant of all."
Mark 9:35

Full disclosure: I love being first. I can't help it. It's as if the need to compete is wired into my DNA. It can even rear its ugly head when I'm in line for confession. It's amazing how annoyed I can become when I'm last in line, and how relieved and perfectly holy I feel when I happen to be first.

Thankfully, Jesus gave us an antidote for this not-so-tiny quirk in our human nature: we are to become servants. He modeled this for us throughout his life, giving the final lesson at the Last Supper and on the cross.

If we apply his example to our own lives, we'll find that the more energy we put into serving others rather than competing with them, the less anxious and more content we will be. I'm going to give it a try!

Lord, deliver me from the desire to be first.

MAY 9

Trust the Lord with all your heart
and lean not on your own understanding;
in all your ways acknowledge him,
and he will direct your paths.
Proverbs 3:5-6 (NIV)

We want to be full, but Jesus says we are blessed in our poverty. We value strength, while the Lord favors brokenness. We seek to be first, as he urges us to be last.

One of the ways to reduce anxiety in our lives is to seek God's will in everything. We experience his greatest peace when we follow his ways. We may not always understand his ways, but that's OK because we don't see things as God does. We can trust that his will is perfect.

It's simple, but it's not easy. God honors our trust in him and his ways. Stepping out in faith may go contrary to our human inclinations or what the world tells us to do, but we cannot fail when we follow the will of God.

Lord, direct my path.

MAY 10

*"You will receive power when the holy Spirit
comes upon you."*
Acts 1:8

Just before he ascended into heaven, Jesus told his followers that they would not be left alone but that the Holy
Spirit would come to them as a helper, guide, and comforter.
Through the Holy Spirit and his power, they would be able to
carry out the mission Jesus gave them to "go into the whole
world and proclaim the gospel to every creature" (Mark 16:15).

That same Holy Spirit is available to us today to help us
accomplish our goals and the good that God wills for our
lives. If we need to break a bad habit, find courage to take a
new job, learn to be assertive, or grow in trust, the Holy Spirit's power can help us.

When we invoke and invite the Holy Spirit, he always comes.

Come, Holy Spirit, come now, come as you wish.

MAY 11

Let each of you look not only to his own interests, but also to the interests of others.
Philippians 2:4 (ESV)

How many times a day do you have to remind yourself to get out of your own head? If you are like me, you camp out there way too often. Our true home, however, is in the heart, where Jesus lives. One of the best ways to move out of the head and into the heart is to consider the needs, wants, and interests of others. Serving our neighbors, family members, coworkers, and even strangers by performing intentional acts of kindness can lift us out of our worries and combat anxiety.

Kindness doesn't cost a penny, but we need to stay alert to the needs of others. A hug, a compliment, a shared sandwich, a smile: for those who feel invisible or alone, you could be the Jesus they need today.

Lord, show me.

MAY 12

"For 'In him we live and move and have our being.'"
Acts 17:28

We do not have everything we need to get through this life—God didn't create us to be self-sufficient. Nor did he create us to be independent from him. We are members of the mystical body of Christ and part of an eternal family. We are never alone. Our days can be long, but life is short, and we can make the most of it when we "live and move and have our being" in the loving embrace of our Lord. He will provide what we are lacking. When Jesus left this earth, he promised to be with us always. He is. Lean on him.

Jesus, walk with me.

MAY 13

The God of all grace . . . will himself restore, confirm,
strengthen, and establish you.
1 Peter 5:10

As I write this book, I am entering a new season of life as a grandmother. Along with the blessings come challenges as I sort through new priorities, roles, and expectations. I am overjoyed, of course, but also somewhat frustrated by the lack of time and energy I seem to have. The limitations are real; "the spirit is willing, but the flesh is weak" (Matthew 26:41).

We will need different graces depending on the season of life we are in. Kindness is a grace and virtue for all seasons, but in the face of our limitations, we need to remember to be kind to ourselves and trust God to replenish us as needed. A good lesson for this great season of life!

Lord, shower me with your grace.

MAY 14

Let your speech always be gracious, seasoned with salt, so that you know how you should respond to each one.
Colossians 4:6

Saying what we mean *to whom we need to say it* is a surefire way to reduce stress in our lives. Being direct and clear in our communication with others is an act of kindness. Speaking the truth in love takes courage, especially when we need to confront someone. But we can learn how to be genuine, gentle, firm, compassionate, clear, and direct. These are skills that will help us in our interactions with others.

The single most important thing we can do in our conversations with others is to "go to the source." Gossip is destructive, and circumventing people when we should speak with them directly does more harm than good. Let's heed the words of the psalmist: "Set a guard, LORD, before my mouth, / keep watch over the door of my lips" (Psalm 141:3). If we guard our mouths, we can become gracious and kind, bringing life and light to others through our speech.

Lord, guard my mouth.

MAY 15

"Do not let your hearts be troubled. You have faith in God;
have faith also in me."

John 14:1

Today is the feast day of St. Dymphna, the patron saint of those with mental or nervous disorders. Ask her to intercede today for people who have endured childhood trauma. Early trauma can be life defining, but faith in God and the help of Jesus can bring healing.

Here is a powerful prayer to St. Dymphna:

Good St. Dymphna, great wonder-worker in every affliction of mind and body, I humbly implore your powerful intercession with Jesus through Mary, the Health of the Sick, in my present need. [Mention your petition.] St. Dymphna, martyr of purity, patroness of those who suffer with nervous and mental afflictions, beloved child of Jesus and Mary, pray to Them for me and obtain my request.

(Pray one Our Father, one Hail Mary and one Glory Be.)[19]

St. Dymphna, virgin and martyr, pray for us.

MAY 16

Cast your care upon the LORD,
who will give you support.
Psalm 55:23

A popular meme offers this insight: "Yesterday is heavy. Put it down." It's a great reminder that we can become accustomed to carrying burdens we were never meant to carry. Yesterday's issues, problems, failures, regrets, confusions, and worries are not meant for today. Wisdom enables us to know the difference between what we should carry forward and what we should leave behind.

Yesterday is done and over. What can you do today, right now, that will lead to a better tomorrow? Right now is all we have. It is all we need to carry, and it is manageable.

Lord, sustain me in this present moment.

MAY 17

*"But show me unfailing kindness like the L*ord*'s kindness
as long as I live."*
1 Samuel 20:14 (NIV)

Being nice and being kind are not the same. In fact, it's been said that niceness is kindness without conviction. Kindness is a virtue, and niceness is not. In most versions of the Bible, the word *nice* doesn't ever appear.

With kindness as our goal, we always consider the welfare of the entire person: mind, body, and soul. St. Edith Stein said, "Do not accept anything as love which lacks truth and do not accept anything as truth which lacks love."[20] A genuine act of kindness is always rooted in love and tells the truth.

Lord, help me to be kind.

MAY 18

As for you, the anointing you received from him remains in you. . . . His anointing teaches you about all things and as that anointing is real, not counterfeit—just as it has taught you, remain in him.

1 John 2:27

There are three conditions that help us to embrace the anointing of the Holy Spirit and remain firmly rooted in him. These are detachment, silence, and docility. Today let's focus on detachment. It calls us to loosen our heartstrings around anything that seems more important to us than God and our relationship with him. It could be an activity, a person, a possession, a talent, an accomplishment, or even a dearly held desire or belief.

The Prayer to Our Lady, Undoer of Knots can help us with inordinate attachments that we need to modify or let go of altogether. (You can find the prayer online.) The Sacrament of Confession is also a good source of grace. The Christian walk is one big lesson in detachment after another. Ask the Holy Spirit: what do I need to let go of?

Lord, I release _____.

MAY 19

My soul, be at rest in God alone,
from whom comes my hope.
Psalm 62:6

When we cultivate interior stillness, we are better able to invite the Holy Spirit into our lives. Attentive to his gentle, subtle movements, we will find him in the deepest recesses of our being.

We need silence because the Holy Spirit speaks softly. Our minds are filled with hundreds of voices—a constant din of distraction. The Holy Spirit's voice is tender, sweet, and special, but too often we can't hear him in the midst of our noisy, boisterous lives.

Stillness and silence were Mary's domain. She can show us the way to more fully receiving her Spouse.

Mary, teach me to be quiet in my soul.

MAY 20

"May it be done to me according to your word."
Luke 1:38

God is a gentleman. He doesn't force his way into our hearts or our lives. He stands at the door and knocks. He waits for permission, just as he waited for Mary to offer her fiat, or yes, to him.

We, too, long to offer the same complete yes to God, our Father, that Mary did. Whether we are aware of it or not, this is the deepest longing of our hearts, the one that drives all others.

The more that we can surrender to him, the greater peace we will experience. The more that we can say "May it be done" in our lives, the freer we will be.

Lord, let it be done.

MAY 21

For by grace you have been saved through faith, and this is not from you; it is the gift of God; it is not from works, so no one may boast.
Ephesians 2:8-9

When in doubt, choose grace. The *Catechism of the Catholic Church* defines *grace* as "*favor*, the *free and undeserved help* that God gives us to respond to his call to become children of God, adoptive sons, partakers of the divine nature and of eternal life" (1996). The Holy Spirit opens us up to God's grace in order to heal our souls and make us holy.

We can't force grace, and we can't earn it, but as with any precious gift, we need to guard and treasure it. We do this by following God's will and cooperating with the Holy Spirit. Grace is a potent force that helps us combat fear, doubt, and those things that work against peace in our hearts.

Lord, send down your grace.

MAY 22

Jesus said . . . , "Do not be afraid; just have faith."
Mark 5:36

Jesus spoke the words in today's verse to a man whose daughter had just died. Jesus says the same to us in the tragic circumstances and trials of life. Just believe. Believe that God is in control even in the throes of suffering; believe that he will make something good come out of evil; believe that he can bring truth where once there were lies; believe that there is a loving purpose and a plan even when you can't fathom it.

Believe, and give him your fears.

Lord, I believe.

MAY 23

For she said within herself, If I may but touch his garment,
I shall be whole.
Matthew 9:21 (KJV)

The woman with the hemorrhage is such a beautiful role model for us. Though she suffered for a long time, she persisted and was made whole. She may have tried many different approaches to healing, but ultimately her journey led her to the right place.

This is our prayer, for ourselves and those out there who are struggling—that our journey brings us to Jesus. It's usually not a straight route. Many of us are crawling and clawing our way through crowds of fears and distractions to get to him. It's OK—keep trying and keep stretching.

Know that Jesus goes before you and behind you, journeying with you on your road to health.

Lord, heal me.

MAY 24

Those who guard mouth and tongue
guard themselves from trouble.
Proverbs 21:23

Our words carry the power to destroy. We see this in our culture today, especially in the damaging effects of social media. Our words can kill the reputations and good names of others, a sin against the sixth commandment. How easy it is to use speech carelessly and casually! In this rapid-fire world we live in, our words can reach a huge audience very quickly, not only causing harm, but also coming back to haunt us.

We need to develop the virtue of prudence in our speech. The greater prudence we exercise, the less anxiety we will experience in our social interactions. We can ponder; we can listen; we can filter; we can withhold our opinions. We can guard our mouths and stay out of trouble! Amen.

Lord, keep me quiet.

MAY 25

When you call me, and come and pray to me,
I will listen to you.
Jeremiah 29:12

All of us carry a deep ache within to be known and understood. This need is satisfied when one other person takes the time to get to know us, listening to our story without judgment. For many reasons, though, we may resist telling our stories.

Past betrayals can hold us back from taking the risk to be vulnerable and totally honest with someone else. We may feel that what we have to say is not interesting, worthwhile, or believable. The risk of revealing our deepest selves stirs up fears of rejection or ridicule.

These barriers create a great internal tension between what we need and what we fear. Remember that God knows who we truly are, and he listens. In fact, God is always listening, even when we are silent, afraid to speak because we are too hurt and confused.

Trust that God listens to you and that his listening is a source of healing in your life. Your story matters, and so do you.

Lord, listen.

MAY 26

*And to know the love of Christ that surpasses knowledge, so
that you may be filled with all the fullness of God.*
Ephesians 3:19

Christian meditation brings us into the divine life of the
Holy Trinity. Going to Eucharistic Adoration is a beautiful
example. Jesus is present in the monstrance as we encounter
him in his humblest form. Our minds cannot comprehend
this mystery, but while we are in his presence, Jesus speaks to
our hearts.

He is the One who fills us and he is our focus. Don't worry
if you can't settle down in your thoughts or if you feel very little while you are there. Trust that Jesus is healing you because
he is . . . one visit at a time.

Lord, fill me.

MAY 27

Worry weighs down the heart,
but a kind word gives it joy.
Proverbs 12:25

"I always mess things up!" "You never listen to me!" These are just two examples of the all-or-nothing statements we have rolling around in our heads all day. Psychologists call it cognitive distortion, and it is common in people who struggle with anxiety or panic. How can we modify these messages so that they don't become the norm? My husband and I have a rule that we learned in our Pre-Cana class over thirty years ago: we don't use the words *always* or *never* when we are angry with one another. This has worked well for us. When we catch one another using a phrase containing *always* or *never,* we immediately joke about it.

Always or never statements are rarely helpful. Stopping to think about what we are really feeling or really want to say will improve our communication and empower us in the process. Try it.

Lord, help me to choose my words wisely.

MAY 28

"Amen, amen, I say to you, unless a grain of wheat falls to the ground and dies, it remains just a grain of wheat; but if it dies, it produces much fruit."
John 12:24

God has beautiful fruit that he wants to raise up out of your pain and struggles. You may have experienced division and despair, but from your sorrow, he can bring unity and harmony. He will plant seeds of goodness and sow hope in your heart; he will bring new life to those places that have died within you. As with any growth, it may take time. There are seasons to our healing, but his harvest is sure.

Lord, bring forth your fruit.

MAY 29

Be not just to excess, and be not overwise.
Why work your own ruin?
Ecclesiastes 7:16

Today's verse is a signature one for the blessing of balance. Balance is always the goal in the spiritual life—and in our physical world as well. We strive for work-life balance, for moderation in our emotions, for a reasonable distribution of the energy we expend on ourselves and others. We strive for equilibrium as we carry out our daily responsibilities. So why do we feel like we are on a tightrope all the time?

Usually, it's because we are holding on too tightly to something. Maybe we're clinging to a relationship, or we're overly attached to a pet project or cause. Sometimes our motivations are not clear or are more self-serving than they should be. Taking a hard look at what might be disrupting balance in our lives is essential. What seems good, righteous, or wise on the surface might be the thing that is undermining our balance and disrupting our peace.

Lord, show me the way to a blessed balance.

MAY 30

"Do to others whatever you would have them do to you."
Matthew 7:12

Those who are at war with others are not at peace with themselves. We all know people who are difficult and cause us stress. We have options when it comes to dealing with them. Sometimes charity dictates that we walk away; other times we may be called to reach out and show compassion. Compassion means to "suffer with" someone.

Christ asks us, as his followers, to be kind to those who are not kind. It's easier to do this when we recognize that each one of us is someone else's "difficult person"!

Lord, help me to perfect the golden rule.

MAY 31

THE VISITATION OF THE BLESSED VIRGIN MARY
*"The Mighty One has done great things for me,
and holy is his name."*
Luke 1:49

Mary spoke the words in today's verse in the company of her cousin Elizabeth as they shared the blessed news that they were both to become mothers. Surely their hearts were bursting with awe and joy. Parenthood is certainly a gift, filled with the highest highs and the lowest lows. When we love so intently and intimately, we cannot help but be subject to intense emotions. This is the risk and vulnerability of love, especially a mother's love.

We can make peace with our emotions. We can receive them as blessings and honor them while not letting them rule us. We don't have to be afraid or ashamed of them or let them linger longer than they should. We can feel our feelings deeply, without apology or judgment, and then by grace we can give them wings and let them go.

*Mary, help me to receive the gift of my emotions
as God intends.*

JUNE

JUNE 1

Though my flesh and my heart fail,
God is the rock of my heart, my portion forever.
Psalm 73:26

June is the month of the Sacred Heart of Jesus, the source of all goodness. In the Sacred Heart, we contemplate the physical heart of Jesus as the source of the divine love that flows continuously, nourishing us all.

St. Margaret Mary Alacoque, to whom Jesus revealed his heart in 1673, said,

> Take up your abode in the loveable heart of Jesus and therein you will find imperturbable peace and the strength to carry out the good desires he gives you. Bring to this divine Heart all of your troubles and afflictions, for whatever emanates from the Sacred Heart is sweet: It changes everything into love.[21]

Consider how you can join Jesus in the safe space of his heart.

Jesus, I rest in you.

JUNE 2

Guard my life and rescue me;
do not let me be put to shame,
for I take refuge in you.
Psalm 25:20 (NIV)

We are good because God says so, but many of us don't believe it. Instead, we believe lies about ourselves, often carried over from childhood. These cause us great shame and cripple our souls, derailing us from God's purpose for our lives.

Jesus is the only One who can deliver and heal us from our shame. We can claim that healing of our inner distortions by taking authority over the lies that bind us. Author Neal Lozano explains that "freedom is found in focusing on Jesus, our savior and deliverer, who has absolute authority over the enemy and who sets us free to know the love of the Father."[22]

Shifting our focus to Jesus will need to be a conscious, daily choice. Shame lives in the darkness, but Jesus brings goodness and light.

Lord, I claim my true identity in you.

JUNE 3

Indeed, goodness and mercy will pursue me
all the days of my life.
Psalm 23:6

According to the *Catechism,* "The practice of goodness is accompanied by spontaneous spiritual joy and moral beauty" (2500). Awesome! So the more we let the virtue of goodness seep into our souls, the greater capacity we have for joy and the more we can appreciate the true beauty that surrounds us in this life.

When goodness becomes habitual and when we experience it as second nature, the world comes alive with vibrancy and joy. This is what God wants for us. Put goodness into practice today.

Lord, let there be goodness in all my days.

JUNE 4

You are my shelter; you guard me from distress.
Psalm 32:7

Corrie ten Boom, a Dutch Christian who helped protect
Jews during World War II, said that the "safest place is in
the center of God's will."[23] She didn't live a "safe" life by any
stretch of the imagination—the Nazis arrested her and sent
her to a concentration camp. The safety she was talking about
is the assurance and peace that come from knowing Jesus and
loving and following his ways.

His will is a firm foundation, a mighty fortress, and a pro-
tective shield for our souls. This kind of safety is what we all
long for. Knowing this, the devil tries to confuse us about right
and wrong, good and evil. He wants to destroy our efforts to
pursue God's will.

Today, walk in God's will, seek him, and cling to the good.
You are safe in his sight.

Lord, protect me.

JUNE 5

I will give you a new heart . . . .
I will remove the heart of stone from your flesh and give you
a heart of flesh.
Ezekiel 36:26

Who among us doesn't need a new heart from time to time? We can be weary of heart, hard of heart, broken-hearted, coldhearted, or suffering from heartache. Life has a way of taking its toll on our hearts. What condition is your heart in today? Know that you can get a total transplant or a partial repair because God is the healer of all hearts. Let him examine your heart today and give you the prognosis. With him, the outcome will always be excellent and full of hope.

Lord, heal my heart.

JUNE 6

The Lord loves righteousness and justice;
the earth is full of his unfailing love.
Psalm 33:5 (NIV)

If you are looking for the best in others, you will find it; if you are looking for the worst, you will find that, too. The same is true of our world. We can focus on all that is wrong or we can believe today's verse: the earth is full of God's unfailing love. Let's seek it. Look for evidence of God's love today.

Lord, show me.

JUNE 7

They that hope in the L<small>ORD</small> *will renew their strength,*
they will soar on eagles' wings;
They will run and not grow weary,
walk and not grow faint.
Isaiah 40:31

Someone once said, "The highest mountains we ever climb are the ones between our ears." Life's hurdles and roadblocks start as tiny thoughts such as *I can't, I shouldn't,* or *I'm not good enough.* They grow into the larger-than-life impasses that keep us from reaching the goals and dreams that we hold dear.

Remember today that you are meant to soar. As the eagle rises above mountain passes, so can you. God may not remove the mountains in your mind or your life, but he will give you the strength to rise above them.

Lord, help me soar.

JUNE 8

"Rejoice and be glad."
Matthew 5:12

Someone once said that when she is feeling anxious, she imagines Jesus sitting next to her and speaking directly to her as he shares a story from the Bible. The Sermon on the Mount (see Matthew 5:1-12) would be a beautiful and helpful passage for anyone who wants to try this exercise.

Even though you may have heard the Sermon on the Mount hundreds of times, try placing yourself right next to Jesus. Open your heart and mind to him and notice the words or phrases that impress you the most. Have a conversation with him in your heart, and let him share with you his lessons of love.

Lord, speak to me.

JUNE 9

I have stilled my soul.
Psalm 131:2

Psalm 131 is like a spiritual lullaby. It entreats us to lay down the thoughts and concerns that are too heavy to carry and invites us to rest in God's arms like a weaned child with its mother. There is no need for us to do anything, no need to perform. There is only the joy of being held in the completeness of God's embrace.

> Lord, my heart is not proud;
>   nor are my eyes haughty.
> I do not busy myself with great matters,
>   with things too sublime for me.
> Rather, I have stilled my soul,
> Like a weaned child to its mother,
>   weaned is my soul. (Psalm 131:1-2)

Lord, hold me.

JUNE 10

The Spirit of the one who raised Jesus from the dead dwells in you.

Romans 8:11

We can carry around a lot of "dead weight" both physically and emotionally without even realizing it. We can remain physically overweight as a means of personal protection and security against past trauma. Our anxieties and worries can bury us and keep us from living life to the full.

For a long time, I was afraid to shed my extra weight. Then one day I made the decision to enter a gym. I was terrified and even cried during my first meeting with the trainer, but I knew that I was finally ready to let go.

Losing weight over a period of a year and a half was like being raised from the dead. As I grew in physical strength and leanness, I became more aware, more engaged, and way less stressed. I experienced the connection between body and spirit—how taking care of our body affects our emotions and interior life. I claimed life over death. You can too.

Lord, live in me.

JUNE 11

Be renewed in the spirit of your minds,
and put on the new self.
Ephesians 4:23-24

Everybody deserves a second chance, and St. Paul is the poster child for that truth. He spent some of his adult life persecuting and killing Christians. He was certain he was doing the right thing until Jesus met him on the road to Damascus to initiate his total transformation.

Paul could have resisted, but he didn't. Instead, he became physically blind for three days, during which time he developed a teachable and reachable spirit. He allowed God to completely renew his mind and change his heart. God can do the same for us if we let him.

Lord, transform me.

JUNE 12

Bear one another's burdens.
Galatians 6:2

Jim prays one simple prayer each morning: "Lord, use me." Then he goes about his business with an expectant heart, treating his everyday life of ordinary encounters as a mission field. He explains that he doesn't have time to go to some faraway land to minister to those who are hungry, broken, or poor. He finds such souls right next to him in church, at the grocery store, and in his family.

Every encounter with another person carries great potential. Jesus loves every person who crosses your path and offers you the opportunity to share his love with them in whatever way you can. How will you carry out your mission today?

Lord, use me.

JUNE 13

FEAST OF ST. ANTHONY OF PADUA
*First of all, then, I ask that supplications, prayers,
petitions, and thanksgivings be offered for everyone.*
1 Timothy 2:1

Sweet St. Anthony, holy helper and finder of lost things and people, you never fail in your mission. I call upon you whenever I am searching for things large or small. When I need to find strength, courage, and hope—or a set of car keys—I know you are listening to my plea, ready to come to my assistance.

I entrust to you those for whom I pray—the lost who need to find their way back home to Jesus, the addicted, those questioning their faith, those who have angrily rejected God. By your intercession, may they find their way to the truth. St. Anthony, I thank God for your spiritual friendship and constant care.

St. Anthony, please come around.

JUNE 14

But the plan of the LORD stands forever,
the designs of his heart through all generations.
Psalm 33:11

God is in control, and his triumph over darkness and evil is assured. We can claim that victory no matter what is going on in our lives. A mother who lost two children to a devastating disease has done this and wards off bitterness and despair by living every moment to the fullest. Another mother whose son was killed by a drunk driver has turned the tide and offered forgiveness to the perpetrator, bringing life back into her own heart.

God will save us from the wages of sin and death. His plan unfolds in our lives in the midst of our struggles. Cling to him and claim the victory even if you cannot see it yet.

Jesus, I trust your plan.

JUNE 15

"My soul magnifies the Lord."
Luke 1:46 (ESV)

You have a unique and unrepeatable part to play in God's plan. There is no one who can offer what you offer, who sees the world in exactly the same way you see it, or who magnifies the Lord the way you do. No one can take your place.

You don't have to be perfect to magnify the Lord; you just need to be as authentic and sincere as you can be. You will bring Jesus into focus for others simply by being you.

Shine on.

Lord, I magnify you.

JUNE 16

"The words I have spoken to you are spirit and life."
John 6:63

E ven though Jesus is in heaven, he hasn't stopped speaking to you and me. We hear his words of spirit and life at Mass, in Scripture, in prayer, and through the Holy Spirit in the words of others who care about us. Our challenge is to filter out the noise so that we can discern what Jesus is saying. This takes time and practice.

Set aside some regular listening time. Read a verse in Scripture or a paragraph in a devotional book and ponder it. Take five or ten minutes of quiet prayer at lunchtime or have a heartfelt conversation with a trusted friend. Develop your own way to start the conversation. Jesus is waiting.

Lord, speak to me.

JUNE 17

"But I say to you, love your enemies,
and pray for those who persecute you."
Matthew 5:44

Jesus doesn't ask us to do the impossible. When he tells us to love our enemies, he is fully prepared to send his grace and our helper, the Holy Spirit, to give us the strength to do this. Forgiving others is so vitally important to our mental, physical, and spiritual well-being that Jesus modeled it from the cross for us: "Father, forgive them, they know not what they do" (Luke 23:34). Forgiveness is a process. Be patient with yourself, but be persistent in pursuing the freedom that comes from forgiving others.

Lord, make me merciful.

JUNE 18

"Blessed is the one who trusts in the LORD,
whose confidence is in him."
Jeremiah 17:7 (NIV)

If you have a problem with self-confidence, pursue God confidence instead. Focus on the strengths, stability, favor, and blessings that he bestows on you. Thank him for providing you with everything that you need to succeed. Today's passage from Jeremiah is powerful. It continues:

"They will be like a tree planted by the water
  that sends out its roots by the stream.
It does not fear when heat comes;
  its leaves are always green.
It has no worries in a year of drought
  and never fails to bear fruit." (Jeremiah 17:8, NIV)

The image of a firmly planted tree that withstands any type of circumstance is the image of every person who is deeply rooted in trust and confidence in God. That person can be you.

Lord, I am rooted in you.

JUNE 19

We all fall short in many respects.
James 3:2

It's good to remember that we all need healing from something, and we may not always put our best foot forward. It takes tremendous energy, compassion, and time to overcome life's obstacles. One way we can help others—and ourselves—is to make sure that our expectations are reasonable and respectful.

Too often we place added pressure on ourselves by imposing unrealistic timelines or holding on to the notion that we (or someone else) should "just get over it." You may have noticed that God doesn't seem to be in a hurry when it comes to this sort of interior healing. Maybe we shouldn't be either.

Lord, guide my expectations.

JUNE 20

"So be perfect, just as your heavenly Father is perfect."
Matthew 5:48

The seventh step of the Twelve Step programs says, "We humbly ask God to remove our shortcomings." In the Act of Contrition, we pray, "I firmly resolve with the help of your grace to sin no more." Both statements confirm that God is an active partner on our way to completion in him. He doesn't leave us adrift to fend for ourselves. Whenever we focus our energy and effort on receiving his grace or surrendering to him, we won't go wrong.

Our perfection is much more God's business than ours. We provide the "grit," the spiritual elbow grease, but he provides the grace. We do our best, we strive for holiness, but ultimately, it is our surrender and trust in him that matter most.

Lord, help me to be holy.

JUNE 21

You know when I sit and stand;
you understand my thoughts from afar.
Psalm 139:2

For some of us, the idea that God knows our every thought might not be so comforting. Our thoughts can be exhausting, embarrassing, or incriminating . . . but wait! God is not scrutinizing our every thought so that he can criticize or accuse us. Instead, he is a great encourager who wants to give us peace of mind.

We don't have to hide anything from God—in fact, we can't. But even though he knows our thoughts, he never condemns us. This shows us how deeply he loves us. There is *no* condemnation in Christ. He knows us, and he loves us.

Lord, purify my mind.

JUNE 22

Be free, yet without using freedom as a pretext for evil.
1 Peter 2:16

The freedom that God gives us is authentic and will always lead us in the right direction. It is the freedom to do the right thing for ourselves and others. In him, we will know the truth, and the truth will set us free. Jesus was clear about his mission when he said,

> "The Spirit of the LORD is on me,
>   because he has anointed me
>   to proclaim good news to the poor.
> He has sent me to proclaim freedom for the prisoners
>   and recovery of sight for the blind,
> to set the oppressed free." (Luke 4:18, NIV)

What do you need from Jesus to live as a person who is free?

Lord, I claim your freedom.

JUNE 23

Be angry but do not sin.
Ephesians 4:26

The Bible doesn't tell us that we must never get angry. We will surely get angry, but when we do, we mustn't let our anger fester, morph into a hardened heart, or lead us into sin.

In fact, anger is an important emotion. Even Jesus got angry. We need anger to inform us and protect us when someone violates our boundaries. Righteous anger inspires necessary changes that can bring about greater good. Stuffing angry feelings does the opposite: it keeps us stuck, creates resentment, and tempts us to a sinful state.

With the Holy Spirit's help, we can accept our angry feelings, acknowledge them without fear, and learn how to express them so that something better follows.

Holy Spirit, show me the way.

JUNE 24

The Nativity of St. John the Baptist
*I believe I shall see the Lord's goodness
in the land of the living.*
Psalm 27:13

John the Baptist was a great proclaimer. He had the greatest news of all tucked inside his heart, and at the right time, in the right place, he announced it to anyone who would listen. He fulfilled his calling by following the promptings of the Spirit within him, thus preparing the way for people to receive Jesus.

We can proclaim the good news too. We can speak of light instead of darkness, of life instead of death. We can see only the bad around us or we can see the goodness of the Lord. The choice is ours. What will you proclaim?

Lord, I will speak of your goodness in the land of the living.

JUNE 25

For freedom Christ set us free; so stand firm and do not
submit again to the yoke of slavery.

Galatians 5:1

L iving a life of devotion to God is essential for living in
freedom. The more we love him and his ways, the freer
we are. The "lesser loves" in our lives can enslave us, but when
we turn away from them, Jesus meets us and brings us out of
our captivity.

Pope St. John Paul II said,

> When freedom does not have a purpose, when it does not wish
> to know anything about the rule of law engraved on the hearts
> of men and women, when it does not listen to the voice of con-
> science, it turns against humanity and society.[24]

We have seen these prophetic words come to pass in today's
world. Ask Jesus to show you the way to authentic freedom.

Jesus, set me free.

JUNE 26

Two are better than one,
because they have a good return for their labor.
Ecclesiastes 4:9 (NIV)

Fear is a heavy load. Sometimes we need other human beings to help us carry our fears. They may not be able to make our fears go away, but they can be with us on the journey. We need to speak our secrets, laugh out loud, go shopping, or pray together. We need someone to listen and not run away, tell us the truth, and reveal their fears to us.

God made us this way—to need each other and to seek out a safe and genuine connection with one another. Our souls long for this kind of union and healing help. If you feel alone and unable to share your fears with anyone, ask the Lord to send you someone. Be open and on the lookout; he will provide.

Lord, send me a friend.

JUNE 27

The righteous holds to his way,
the one with clean hands increases in strength.

Job 17:9

If you were in a wrestling match with God over your worries, who would win? Isn't it true that we can sometimes hold on to our fears for dear life? God wants to relieve the burden of our worries and anxieties, but we can have a hard time giving them up. What would you do if you didn't worry? How would you spend your time? What would you do with your energy?

If someone throws us a lifeline, we often need to let go of something else in order to grab it. What do you need to release in order to grab hold of God's lifeline?

Lord, rescue me.

JUNE 28

Faith is the realization of what is hoped for and evidence of things not seen.
Hebrews 11:1

When my grandson went missing for a short time, I put out a mass text to all the prayer warriors I know. One response struck me deeply: "Awaiting in faith the news of his safe return." Those words immediately calmed my spirit. Faith works. It activates hope. It gives us confidence and assures us that God is always in control.

Life is full of uncontrollable and unforeseen situations, yet a prayer of faith is a powerful force. We anticipate what we hope for, and we put into practice what we believe: that God is good all the time, no matter what happens.

Thank you, Lord, for the gift of faith.

JUNE 29

"All things are possible for God."
Mark 10:27

Our God is the God of the impossible. We often forget this when we are crushed in spirit, but it's true. When we suffer, he asks only that we turn to him. If we don't have the energy to do even that, then all we need to do is rest in him. We should feel free to collapse into his arms. He's there for us.

All goodness flows from God. He's the source of our goodness, and to him we give unending glory: in him all things are possible. Let us thank him!

Thanks be to God!

JUNE 30

*Yet when you seek the LORD, your God, . . . you shall indeed
find him if you search after him with all your
heart and soul.*

Deuteronomy 4:29

Finding God brings peace to our souls. I remember when
I was mourning many losses in my life. I was missing my
parents and several friends who had passed on. I longed to
have some sign that they were all OK and somehow able to
hear my prayers. I became quite bold in asking God for this
sign: I asked him to send me a feather.

The next day I was crossing the street to go to my office.
In my path, sticking straight up from a crack in the sidewalk,
was a seven-inch feather! It was an unmistakable, undeniable
answer to my prayer and also proof that God has a sense of
humor. He wants to be found by us. Seek him.

Lord, reveal your presence.

JULY

JULY 1

*Let perseverance finish its work so that you may be mature
and complete, not lacking anything.*
James 1:4 (NIV)

At first glance, long-suffering and patience seem to be quite similar, but there is a difference. Fr. Lawrence Lovasik, a missionary priest and prolific writer who died in 1986, offered a clear definition of these two virtues: *patience* is "lovingly and fully accepting the trials that Divine Goodness sees fit to let a person undergo," and *long-suffering* is "knowing how to wait, feeling certain during trials, that God's moment will come when He will fully aid the suffering person."[25] With this definition, we could say that patience is the outward sign of an interior state of long-suffering.

The Lord must think that these are important fruits to cultivate, because every day we encounter opportunities to grow in patience and long-suffering! In fact, today's verse reveals what the big payoff will be as we cultivate the fruit of long-suffering in our lives: we will be mature and complete. That sounds like a worthwhile pursuit to me!

Lord, teach me to wait well.

JULY 2

Be strong and take heart, all who hope in the LORD.
Psalm 31:25

Someone in great anguish wrote Psalm 31. Presumably it was David who put into words, throughout the psalms, what it feels like to be under great stress. Earlier the psalmist said:

Though I had said in my alarm,
   "I am cut off from your eyes."
Yet you heard my voice, my cry for mercy,
   when I pleaded with you for help. (Psalm 31:23)

Anxiety can make us feel "cut off from [God's] eyes," unable to sense his love and comfort. The psalmist, in such times, recalls the good times when God showed his faithfulness and presence. He may not be able to feel it, but he can *remember* when God was near.

Paraphrased, I'd put it this way: "Lord, I feel awful right now and I hate it, but I know you are here because you have heard my voice and helped me in the past. I just need you to do it again . . . and hurry up!"

Lord, I remember that you are near.

JULY 3

*The Father of compassion and God of all
encouragement . . . encourages us in our every affliction,
so that we may be able to encourage those who are in any
affliction with the encouragement with which we ourselves
are encouraged by God.*
2 Corinthians 1:3-4

Today's verse helps us to understand the potential benefits
of our suffering and difficulties in life. God allows us to
experience them so that we can know his great love, encouragement, and compassion. In turn, we take the consolation we
have received and share it with others. God uses hurting people to help hurting people. As we bring to others the comfort
and assistance we have received, we pay it forward. In doing
so, our pain is never in vain.

Lord, encourage me.

JULY 4

Now the Lord is the Spirit, and where the Spirit of the Lord is, there is freedom.
2 Corinthians 3:17

In Christ we have the hope that we can be truly free. Yet before we can be free, we must know how we are bound. We all have a lifelong vulnerability to sin—the Church calls this "concupiscence." The *Catechism* says, "As a result of original sin, human nature is weakened in its powers; subject to ignorance, suffering, and the domination of death; and inclined to sin (This inclination is called 'concupiscence.')" (418).

Many people believe that there is no such thing as sin, or if there is, there are no consequences when we sin. As a result, sin has enslaved us even more, it seems, in our hyperconnected world.

Sin undermines us by fueling our fears and interfering with our judgment. We need to take it to Confession, where God's mercy reaches out to us in absolution. True freedom flows from the heart of God, through the Holy Spirit, in the confessional. Receive that freedom today.

Lord, set me free.

JULY 5

As an example of suffering and patience, brothers, take the prophets who spoke in the name of the Lord. Behold, we consider those blessed who remained steadfast.
James 5:10-11 (ESV)

Moses exemplified the fruit of long-suffering as he dealt with difficult people. On the way to the Promised Land, he had to contend with the relentless grumbling of the Israelites about everything from the quality of the food to the way he looked when he came down from the mountain. Then there were their constant distractibility and penchant for worshipping false idols. His own siblings openly criticized him, turning others against him because they didn't like the woman he married.

How did Moses respond? He wore himself out praying and pleading with God on their behalf. Maybe that's why we say, "Holy Moses!"

Walking away when your overtired spouse tries to pick a fight or resisting the temptation to retaliate are all examples of longsuffering. Take heart. You are one step closer to the promised land of detachment and freedom in your soul.

Lord, help!

JULY 6

Even if my father and mother forsake me,
the Lord will take me in.
Psalm 27:10

Because we live in a fallen world, we might not have received the love, attachment, or sense of security in childhood that we needed in order to feel safe in the world. To cope, we become hypervigilant, oversensitive, or chronically anxious—a carryover from childhood that becomes our norm as adults.

We can't go back and get what we needed, but we can be healed. Most people discover that physical self-care, emotional support, therapy, medication, prayer, and participation in the sacraments—or any combination of those—can bring freedom and wholeness.

What are you missing that God can provide? Ask him in prayer to show you what you needed but didn't receive in your childhood or at another time in your life. Ask him to fill that hole in your soul. He will.

Lord, show me.

JULY 7

Anyone who approaches God must believe that he exists and that he rewards those who seek him.

Hebrews 11:6

What do you believe about God? If you believe that he is a hard taskmaster or an uninterested or critical bystander, then you are not likely to seek him, believe that he cares, or trust that he wants to make your life better. Do you believe that he rewards those who seek him?

Today's verse tells us that if we seek God, he will be found, and he will reward us. We often blame God when something goes wrong in our lives, but when things go well, we are slow to believe in God's reward. Seek God and expect to find him throughout your day, knowing he has something good in store for you.

Lord, reward me.

JULY 8

I can do all things through him who strengthens me.
Philippians 4:13 (ESV)

We plan, we prepare, and still—life happens. Anything from a curve ball to a "cut you to the knees" kind of disaster can remind us that most things are completely out of our control. Sometimes a difficult situation becomes a season of suffering that threatens to overtake us.

In all these circumstances, we can cling to and claim today's verse. Be comforted in knowing that Jesus never leaves your side. He provides the strength. It doesn't matter how weak or ill equipped or overwhelmed you may feel inside; Jesus will not withhold his grace to get you through.

Even in our everyday lives when things seem to be going smoothly, we can feel overwhelmed by a task or responsibility. Repeating today's verse throughout the day is a good reminder that will help us stay on course. In Jesus, we have a power source that can never be depleted.

Lord, strengthen me.

JULY 9

I consider that the sufferings of this present time are as nothing compared with the glory to be revealed for us.
Romans 8:18

Have you ever considered that the beauty of life lies in the nitty-gritty, messy moments? Those moments when we are barely hanging on—when an unexpected loss hits us like a punch in the gut, or the pieces of a shattered relationship are scattered at our feet. It's very possible that without moments of sheer panic, we would never seek God's peace. Without experiencing betrayals, we would never test the fidelity of his heart; without our deepest wounds, we would not yearn for his healing love.

Jesus didn't spare himself a single moment of suffering while he was on earth. He invites us to take up our cross because he knows that the Father can and will bring meaning and victory through it. God can make the messy moments of our lives matter the most when we let go of our fairy-tale endings and follow him.

Father, I will consider that my present suffering is bringing me a step closer to your glory.

JULY 10

God is faithful; he will not let you be tempted beyond what
you can bear. But when you are tempted, he will also
provide a way out so that you can endure it.
1 Corinthians 10:13 (NIV)

When a priest told Sara that her anxiety was a temptation, not a sin, she felt great relief. The priest encouraged her to unite her anxieties to the cross of Jesus as an offering for the good of others. This turned her temptation into a gift to be given.

Sara began tuning into her anxiety just enough to be able to offer it up before it got the best of her. She still experienced the anxiety, but instead of dreading that it was present, she thanked the Lord for the opportunity to make an offering on behalf of others.

None of us are free of temptations, but we don't have to fear them. God allows them because he is prepared to help us overcome them. Offering them back to him for the sake of others is one way they lose their power over us.

Lord, lead me as I offer up my temptations as prayerful gifts
for others.

JULY 11

[We are] strengthened with every power, in accord with his
glorious might, for all endurance and patience, with joy.
Colossians 1:11

We often want immediate deliverance, but that is not how
we learn to bear temptation. We build up our self-control muscles through practice, trial, and error. When we fail
or fall, we don't need to start over from the beginning. We
simply confess and move on, facing forward, armed with the
lessons and strength we have gathered so far.

We are strengthened one temptation at a time. What do
you need from God—what "power"—in order to overcome
temptation? Ask the Holy Spirit to provide it.

Holy Spirit, help me.

JULY 12

Be firm, steadfast, always fully devoted to the work of the Lord, knowing that in the Lord your labor is not in vain.
1 Corinthians 15:58

The Lord is pleased when we consecrate our work to him, no matter how mundane or challenging. He cares about our comings and goings—a day devoted to him is never wasted. His kingdom is established in us one daily duty at a time, completed out of love and obedience. God is not looking for grandiose accomplishments. Whatever is right in front of us today is the thing we're called to do.

Lord, I labor for love of you.

JULY 13

We have this hope as an anchor for the soul.
Hebrews 6:19 (NIV)

I love the image of Jesus sleeping in the boat during the storm (see Mark 4:38-40). When life gets overwhelming for me, I take a nap too. If Jesus does it, then I don't have to feel guilty about it! But the other reason I find the sleeping Jesus such a comfort is that I know I can always join him, in spirit, in the boat.

I can call on him, rest in him, sit still, choose trust, have faith, and be anchored in the hope he provides. Jesus can stop the storms in our lives at any time, but often he doesn't because he is teaching us how to weather them.

Lord, anchor me.

JULY 14

For those who are led by the Spirit of God are
children of God.
Romans 8:14

What does it mean to be led by the Spirit? Joyce compared it to "putting on a new pair of shoes that goes
only when God says to go." She said that now she can sense
the difference between stepping out in front of God or allowing him to lead the way. Her daily surrender to the Spirit has
replaced her inner fears about what might happen next with a
sense of delight in waiting for God's will to unfold in her life.

Joyce discovered that allowing herself to be led by the Spirit
brought life into balance and, with that balance, a steady measure of peace. "It's like the difference between the rushing
rapids and the meandering river in your spirit," she explained.
Sounds like a good way to go through life!

Holy Spirit, lead me.

JULY 15

"And I will be a father to you,
and you shall be sons and daughters to me, "
says the Lord Almighty.
2 Corinthians 6:18

When my granddaughter was born, I was reminded of how much a human heart can love. Holding her in my arms, counting her little fingers and toes, brought back all the memories of how life changing love can be. It's hard for us to believe, but God our Father loves us infinitely more than even our greatest experience of love here on earth.

This is how he loves us:

> "Are not two sparrows sold for a small coin? Yet not one of them falls to the ground without your Father's knowledge. Even all the hairs of your head are counted. So do not be afraid; you are worth more than many sparrows." (Matthew 10:29-31)

Such an intimate bond our Father God has with us—he counts the hairs on our heads! The truth is that God is deeply in love with you, and there is nothing you can do about it.

Father, thank you for loving me.

JULY 16

Your word is a lamp for my feet,
a light for my path.
Psalm 119:105

Healing rarely happens in a straight line. We can be going on our merry way and then *boom*, we encounter a setback that threatens to take us off course. But a setback is just a step back. As one saying has it, an optimist is someone who figures that taking a step backward after taking a step forward is not a disaster but more like a cha-cha.

It's OK to feel lost, to take a wrong turn. It's OK to not know where we are going. Our guide is the Holy Spirit. He knows our desired destination, but he rarely turns on the high beams along the way. Usually, he illuminates just enough of the path so that we can take the next step. That's all we need. Meandering is good for the soul that is on the road to healing.

Holy Spirit, guide me.

JULY 17

For our boast is this, . . . that we have conducted ourselves
in the world, . . . with the simplicity and sincerity of God.
2 Corinthians 1:12

You can be exactly who you are today; you don't have to be anybody else. You don't have to try to be smarter, funnier, friendlier, or happier, or anything that you are not. Give yourself permission to just "be." When someone asks you how you are, tell them honestly. Be real; be you. Let go of the need to please or impress other people by being someone different than who you are. Stay true to you and how God made you, without apology or alteration.

Authenticity is a gift we give ourselves. Being who we are, right now, is all that is required of us. Be you, because no one else can.

Lord, help me to be me.

JULY 18

I ask that supplications, prayers, petitions, and
thanksgivings be offered for everyone, . . . that we may lead
a quiet and tranquil life in all devotion and dignity. This
is good and pleasing to God our savior.
1 Timothy 2:1, 2-3

Keeping it simple is hard for those of us with anxiety, but
it's not impossible. Scripture is full of prescriptions for
living that help us to disengage from the complexity of life.
Today's verse, from St. Paul to his protégé Timothy, is one such
instruction. Let's break it down. Prayer is key. Making prayer
a part of our daily ritual and routine lays a firm foundation.
In particular, praying for others and following up with thanksgiving can keep us grounded. Life is simpler when we focus
less on ourselves and more on helping others.

Finally, St. Paul reminds us that a calm and quiet life is good
and pleasing to God. Replacing drama with devotion is defi-
nitely a good idea.

Lord, help me to keep it simple.

JULY 19

But we also glory in our sufferings, because we know that
suffering produces perseverance; perseverance, character;
and character, hope.
Romans 5:3-4 (NIV)

Of course, we want to avoid suffering. Nobody likes it,
but as Catholics we believe there is a purpose for it and
that our Lord is in solidarity with those who suffer. He is even
known as the Suffering Servant, prefigured in the Book of Isaiah as "pierced for our sins, / crushed for our iniquity" (53:5).

The world tends to see suffering as punishment, but many
saints have commented that Christ is nearer to us when we
suffer than at any other time. Our Lady, too, is said to be a
source of comfort and consolation in times of suffering. She
knew sorrow, and our deep anguish will not scare her away.

Finding the silver lining in our suffering requires grace.
Perseverance is good; character is good; hope is good. So is
saying, "Thank you, Lord." Ask yourself: what good fruit can
come from my suffering?

Lord, help me find the answer.

JULY 20

So whoever is in Christ is a new creation: the old things
have passed away; behold, new things have come.
2 Corinthians 5:17

To cope with our fears, we can fall back into what's known as a "life role." That's our default mode, that person we become when we're trying to hide our real self from others, when we don't want them to see our pain. My friend Patty calls it "putting on the old sweater." The hero, the lost child, the enabler, the perfectionist, and the comedian are all examples. My default mode—the life role I took on as a means of self-protection—is that of the helper.

It's hard to let go of our life roles because they have served us well, and some good has come from them. But just like an old sweater, there comes a time when it no longer fits or becomes unacceptably worn around the edges. Putting it on is no longer comforting—it's constricting or unbecoming.

To let go of this life role, we need to first be aware of it, discover who we are without it, and then release it. This requires love, patience, trust, and vulnerability.

Lord, make me whole.

JULY 21

"I am the vine, you are the branches. Whoever remains in me and I in him will bear much fruit, because without me you can do nothing."

John 15:5

I once heard a saying that has stuck with me: "Don't be afraid to go out on a limb—it's where the fruit is." And Jesus reminds us that when we do, he is with us. Taking appropriate risks, stepping out of the boat, casting our nets into the deep—these are images that encourage us to trust the Lord with our plans and dreams. He is always beckoning us to follow him into the unknown. We can take comfort and courage from the fact that apart from him, we can do nothing. He provides everything we need to be fruitful in our efforts.

Lord, I trust you.

JULY 22

For everything created by God is good, and
nothing is to be rejected.
1 Timothy 4:4

It is tempting to reject the parts of us that we are ashamed of or the past experiences that have caused us pain. But if we reject these things before the Holy Spirit has had a chance to reach us and teach us through what we've endured, we will miss the good that can come from evil. If we avoid facing the pain, we will prolong it and experience unnecessary suffering. If we reject the opportunity to forgive and let go, we will be forever stuck.

The virtue of long-suffering does not mean that we remain in our misery. It means we allow Jesus to redeem us through it.

Lord, redeem me.

JULY 23

*[Jesus] said, "I tell you truly, this poor widow put in more
than all the rest; for those others have all made offerings
from their surplus wealth, but she, from her poverty, has
offered her whole livelihood."*
Luke 21:3-4

One good reason to work through our fears and anxieties
is that they can interfere with our ability to be generous.
The widow in today's verse was poor in the things of this world,
but rich in the things of God. Depleted materially, she could
not be depleted spiritually. She was full of what mattered most:
trust, faith, and the freedom to give from her heart.

It is better "to give than to receive," as St. Paul says in the
Acts of the Apostles (20:35). In giving, our hearts expand and
our fears diminish. Giving in spite of our needs will fill us up.

Lord, free me to give.

JULY 24

"Worthy are you, Lord our God,
to receive glory and honor and power,
for you created all things;
because of your will they came to be and were created."
Revelation 4:11

God's heart beats through the beauty of his creation. When we are overwhelmed, we ground ourselves by taking a walk, looking up at the clouds, or digging in the dirt. God's breath is in the wind; his smile is in the sunset; his embrace is in the rustle of the trees. Discover the part of nature that speaks to your soul. Do you find peace in a waterfall or a mountaintop? Do you delight in flowers or fauna? Are you settled by the sea or sitting by a campfire? Go there. God is waiting.

Lord, I seek your beauty.

JULY 25

"Blessed are they who are persecuted for the sake of righteousness, for theirs is the kingdom of heaven."
Matthew 5:10

Of all the blessings that flow from following Jesus, being persecuted is probably not at the top of your list. But St. Paul leaves no doubt that persecution will be ours: "In fact, all who want to live religiously in Christ Jesus will be persecuted" (2 Timothy 3:12).

Nevertheless, Jesus promised that if we are persecuted for righteousness' sake, then the kingdom of God will be ours. When you feel alone, rejected, or persecuted, cling to a crucifix, and contemplate it. Let Jesus console you, and his kingdom will surely come.

Lord, console me.

JULY 26

Lᴏʀᴅ Almighty,
blessed is the one who trusts in you.
Psalm 84:12 (NIV)

"Jesus, I trust in you" is an effective prayer. Said repeatedly throughout the day, it helps us flex our faith muscles and strengthens our trust. Just as physical conditioning builds us up, repetition in our spiritual practice builds us up over time. If you want to grow in trust, claim it in the name of Jesus. He will prove himself worthy of your confident plea.

Jesus, I trust in you.

JULY 27

Moreover, God is able to make every grace abundant for you,
so that in all things, always having all you need, you may
have an abundance for every good work.
2 Corinthians 9:8

It's OK to ask for help, to let others know what we need and expect that our needs will be met. This is not being selfish; it's being human. We wouldn't dream of ignoring the requests or needs of others, so why would we dismiss or fail to express our own?

The virtue of long-suffering doesn't mean that we disregard our own needs or deny ourselves the feedback and guidance of others. Self-care is an important facet of daily life. It's our duty to preserve the integrity of the self, and that means honoring our human needs with dignity and respect.

Lord, I will honor my needs.

JULY 28

"The LORD is gracious and merciful,
slow to anger and abounding in steadfast love.
Psalm 145:8 (ESV)

If we want to reflect God and share his goodness with others, then we will be slow to anger. God is long-suffering and merciful with us, so we strive to treat others the same way. Yet anger is tricky. It's often referred to as fear's overcoat. In other words, for some, anger is a cover-up for fear. It is easier to be incensed or irritated than to show the vulnerability of feeling afraid. An angry, critical, or judgmental person can be driven by deep-seated insecurities of which she is not aware.

Are you slow to anger? What part does fear play in your ability or inability to hold your temper? How can mercy become a mainstay in your life?

Holy Spirit, enlighten me.

JULY 29

Many are the plans of the human heart,
but it is the decision of the LORD that endures.
Proverbs 19:21

God has a plan and a purpose for each one of us. The more we seek it, the more at peace we will be. Most of life's troubles come when we live outside of God's plan or when someone we love chooses to do so. It's hard to stand by and watch someone suffer the consequences of abandoning God's will for them. People are free to make bad choices, turn to addiction, or walk away from a life of faith and morals.

We can't force anyone to turn back to God. It's something people must do for themselves. It's between the individual and God.

In these circumstances, our most effective course of action—what we are called to do—is this: pray with all our hearts, follow God's purpose for our lives, and trust that God's plan for our loved ones remains in place. It does.

Lord, I trust your plan.

JULY 30

You have taken off the old self with its practices and have put on the new self, which is being renewed.
Colossians 3:9-10

There is something to be said for blank slates: a crisp journal page, a white canvas, the dawn of a new day. Life is full of blank slates and second chances. If we don't like the story of our lives, we can turn a page. If we are looking for a do-over, there is always tomorrow. Feeling burdened by failures, we can go to Confession. Our renewal in grace is a day-by-day happening. Put on your new self and live.

Lord, renew me.

JULY 31

St. Ignatius of Loyola

*Call to me, and I will answer you; I will tell you great
things beyond the reach of your knowledge.*

Jeremiah 33:3

St. Ignatius triumphed over his obsessive-compulsive thoughts
and anxiety through a combination of spiritual exercises
and mental examination. He wrote a prayer that can be a great
help in times of trouble:

O Christ Jesus,
when all is darkness
and we feel our weakness and helplessness,
give us the sense of Your presence,
Your love, and Your strength.
Help us to have perfect trust
in Your protecting love
and strengthening power,
so that nothing may frighten or worry us,
for, living close to You,
we shall see Your hand,
Your purpose, Your will through all things.[26]

St. Ignatius, intercede for us.

AUGUST

AUGUST 1

"For he has looked upon his handmaid's lowliness;
behold, from now on will all ages call me blessed."
Luke 1:48

In August, we contemplate the Immaculate Heart of Mary. We venerate its interior sweetness and the tender love that she has for all of us as her spiritual children. Mary revealed her heart when she appeared to the three children in Fatima, Portugal, in 1917. Her heart was encircled with thorns, a reference to the sins of humanity, and lit by a flame of love.

Mary wants us to know her heart. It's a human heart, like our own, but it's filled with many treasures and graces for us from Jesus. We pray, "Hail Mary, full of grace," and we trust in her generous heart to shower us with those graces when we need them most.

St. Alphonsus Liguori, whose feast day is today, struggled with severe scruples and anxiety. He wrote a prayer asking for five graces: forgiveness, divine light, detachment, confidence in Jesus and Mary, and perseverance. Pray to Mary—she will provide these graces for us from Jesus.

Immaculate Heart of Mary, help me.

AUGUST 2

*With all humility and gentleness, with patience, bearing
with one another through love.*
Ephesians 4:2

Being gentle and humble doesn't come naturally for most of us. We need grace to bear with one another in love and even to bear with ourselves sometimes. Being humble means that we are assured of our dignity and value, free to forego our own interests and lift up others. A humble person doesn't need to prove her worth.

Mary, the mother of Jesus, embodies humility and can help us to grow in this virtue. The more humble we become, the less likely we are to be worried about things we cannot control.

Lord, humble me.

AUGUST 3

"Why do you notice the splinter in your brother's eye, but do not perceive the wooden beam in your own eye?"
Matthew 7:3

Even when Jesus walked the earth, there was no shortage among his disciples of opinions, judgments, comparisons, and finger-pointing. His followers jostled for first place and argued among themselves about who was the greatest. Perhaps it is part of our fallen nature to continuously measure ourselves against others, but there is a better way.

The way of meekness offers freedom from all useless comparisons and concerns about our faults and advantages versus the faults and advantages of others. It allows us to let go of harsh and haughty spirits so that we can live and let live. Meekness is really wisdom in action, a prescription for knowing ourselves and accepting others for who they are.

Lord, help me to live and let live in you.

AUGUST 4

"Oh, that today you would hear his voice, 'Harden not your hearts.'"
Hebrews 3:7

What does a hardened heart look like? Only God knows for sure, but it can manifest itself in outward rigidity or a penetrating coldness from within. It can be a heart that has numbed itself against a tide of uncomfortable emotions or experiences. Over time our hearts can become impenetrable, unable to receive the joy, spontaneity, and peace our Lord wants to give us.

If your heart is starting to get a little crusty around the edges, never fear—the Holy Spirit will come to your aid. He can work on any hard heart and turn it into a "heart of flesh" (Ezekiel 36:26). He can help us to have a heart like Jesus' heart.

Come, Holy Spirit!

AUGUST 5

"Learn from me, for I am meek and humble of heart."
Matthew 11:29

Meekness is not valued these days. Those who are bold, outspoken, uninhibited, and opinionated seem to rule the day. Yet as Christians, we are called to be countercultural, exemplifying the virtue of meekness. It's much needed today as an antidote to the angry agitation that seems so pervasive.

Practicing meekness helps us to grow in the ability to remain calm, cool, and collected in the face of adversity, including the rising tide of our own anger. A meek person has the inner reserve to withhold retaliation when someone wrongs them, as Jesus did when Pontius Pilate accused him and when the guards mocked him.

With Jesus and Mary as our models in meekness, we can see that it's a great strength. In fact, St. John Chrysostom said, "Nothing is more powerful than meekness. For as a fire is extinguished by water, so a mind inflated by anger is subdued by meekness."[27]

Lord, teach me the lesson of your heart
and help me to be meek.

AUGUST 6

Be strong and steadfast; have no fear or dread . . . , for it
is the LORD, your God, who marches with you; he will never
fail you or forsake you.
Deuteronomy 31:6

Bravery and courage are not the same thing, but both play important roles in life.

> Bravery is the ability to confront pain, danger, or attempts of intimidation without any feeling of fear. . . . Courage, on the other hand, is the ability to undertake an overwhelming difficulty or pain despite the eminent and unavoidable presence of fear.[28]

David, when he was fighting Goliath, didn't experience fear. He was brave. Esther, however, was afraid when she confronted the king to save her people, but she fortified herself with prayer and persisted. She valued a greater good over her own safety or comfort. Esther was courageous.

With God by our side, we can be courageous and brave.

Lord, stay by my side.

AUGUST 7

Since we have gifts that differ according to the grace given to us, let us exercise them.
Romans 12:6

We all have our limits. We have limited energy, time, and talent. That's OK. God has gifted you in a unique way so he can fulfill his purpose through you. No one else can do what you are called to do. So don't focus on what you lack; focus on what God has given you. Explore with the Holy Spirit the ways God has equipped you and the ways you can apply your gifts and talents to your circumstances at this time in your life. Each season of life will invite you to a new understanding of how God has blessed you and how you can exercise your gifts for the greater good.

Thank you, God, for your good gifts.

AUGUST 8

*"Do not fear or be dismayed . . .
for the battle is not yours but God's."*
2 Chronicles 20:15

W isdom dictates that we do not have to fight every battle. In fact, there is much truth in the popular advice
to pick and choose your battles.

Choosing our battles gives God time to work in the situation. We can engage in conflict on a selective basis, arrive at a
good solution, and improve our relationships, but only if we
"make space for grace," as my friend Kathy always says. When
we give God the opportunity to infuse his Holy Spirit into our
struggles with others, the results are always good.

Thank you, Father, for being in the midst of my battles.

AUGUST 9

What your hands provide you will enjoy;
you will be blessed and prosper.
Psalm 128:2

Today is the feast day of St. Teresa Benedicta of the Cross—
Edith Stein. Though she was brilliant, Edith struggled with
emotional instability as a child. Driven in her quest for knowledge and truth, she was burned out by the time she was thirteen
years old. She left school and went to live with an older sister.

During this hiatus, Edith spent long hours doing physical
labor in the home. She didn't like housework (who does?), but
she found that the exertion coupled with the mindlessness of
the tasks reduced her stress and cleared her mind.

Manual labor is good therapy. The decreased need for it
might be contributing to the increase in unmanageable stress
levels across society. Washing windows or scrubbing the floor
might be the best medicine for healthy, stress-free living. Edith
would probably agree. Manual work helped to put her back
on track to become the saint we know and love today.

Lord, bless our work.

AUGUST 10

"For the measure with which you measure will in return be measured out to you."

Luke 6:38

In God's economy, the more we give, the more we get back. If we are merciful toward those who have done us wrong, then we will receive an abundance of mercy back. In other words, if we refuse to retaliate against or reject those who truly deserve it, then God will grant us the same consideration and pardon when we fail.

This means that we don't have to worry about getting even or counting the cost. We can only control our own actions and the way that we measure out our lives. As St. Paul says in his Letter to the Galatians, the simple truth is that we reap what we sow (see 6:7). Let's resolve to sow the seeds of mercy.

Lord, I love your ways.

AUGUST 11

Watch carefully then how you live, . . . giving thanks always and for everything in the name of our Lord Jesus Christ to God the Father.
Ephesians 5:15, 20

It's time for a gratitude check! What are you grateful for, both big things and small? Take an inventory of all the ways God has been working in your life, the blessings he has bestowed, the prayers he has answered, and the solutions he has sent your way. And while you are at it, thank him for the road-blocks, wrong turns, and the ways that he is asking you to wait.

We are called to give thanks always and for everything because it is good for our souls. Applying gratitude to any situation is like drawing a big, bright red X over our worries and agitations. Try it.

Lord, I am grateful.

AUGUST 12

*Beloved, I hope you are prospering in every respect and are
in good health, just as your soul is prospering.*
3 John 1:2

Someone described depression and anxiety as "cancers of
the mind," and for some of us, they are diseases that need
medical treatment. There's no shame in either the disease
or seeking treatment. We're not weak or defective. Speaking
out about our internal struggles can reduce the stigma, but
we don't have to if we don't want to. Our stories are our own,
and we can do with them what we will.

There are no hard-and-fast rules for recovery. Everybody's
route to wholeness is different. Jesus is with you on that route.
Be open and seek help when you need it.

Lord, lead me.

AUGUST 13

Always be ready to give an explanation to anyone who asks you for a reason for your hope, but do it with gentleness and reverence.
1 Peter 3:15-16

Many people worry about their loved ones who are away from the Church. Parents are concerned that their children will lose their faith when they leave for college, and grandparents lament the world their grandchildren have inherited. The moral decline of our culture weighs heavily on all families striving to live holy lives. The Church itself is struggling to draw people back who have fallen away.

Today's verse tells us what to do and how to do it. We don't have to change anyone's mind, convince, or cajole. We just need to share our hope and what Jesus has done in our lives. Tell others what he means to you, but do so in a spirit of gentleness and reverence. He will do the rest.

Lord, fill me with hope.

AUGUST 14

St. Maximilian Kolbe
*Even though I walk through the valley of the shadow of death,
I will fear no evil, for you are with me.*
Psalm 23:4

St. Maximilian Kolbe died at the Auschwitz concentration camp during World War II. He offered himself in place of another prisoner who had been selected to die in a starvation bunker, along with nine others, in retaliation for the escape of a fellow prisoner. Maximilian endured to the end until the guards finally killed him by lethal injection. He is the patron saint of drug addicts because of the manner of his death, and he is a powerful intercessor for all hurting people.

Every addicted person is fueled by fears that can be healed. Common fears include fear of failure, fear of what life without addiction will be like, fear of change, fear of rejection, fear of discomfort from withdrawal, and fear of success.

Do some of these fears sound familiar? Take time today to consider which fears might be in the driver's seat of your life, and ask St. Maximilian to help you kick them to the curb. He's a good companion for your journey.

St. Maximilian, be with me.

AUGUST 15

A great sign appeared in heaven: a woman clothed with the sun, with the moon under her feet and a crown of twelve stars on her head.

Revelation 12:1 (NIV)

Today we celebrate the feast of the Assumption of Mary, that moment when the mother of Jesus was taken body and soul into heaven. Her yes at the Annunciation carried her through the darkest hours of pain and loss back to him in this glorious feast marking her entry into heaven. Her last recorded words were "Do whatever he tells you" (John 2:5). These are our marching orders, the instructions Mary leaves with us today. If we follow them, our yes will also bring us to him.

You might wonder what Jesus is telling you to do. It's usually nothing out of the ordinary—a call to faithfully fulfill your daily duties as Mary did. Most of us lead hidden lives just as she did, lives of quiet obedience and tender love. This is the way of meekness, the way of Mary. Say yes and follow Jesus through her.

Jesus, my yes is yours forever.

AUGUST 16

Haughtiness brings humiliation,
but the humble of spirit acquire honor.
Proverbs 29:23

Florence was down and out and often wandered through town searching dumpsters for something to eat. Watching her day after day tore at my heart, so I invited her into my office for a meal. She graciously accepted.

Florence's clothes were soiled and torn, and her hands were caked with dirt, yet she sat before me with a sense of self-possession. She spoke very little, but she was polite and responsive to my attempts to begin a conversation. When the food arrived, I asked Florence if she wanted to wash her hands. She asked if I could help her. I ended up washing her hands and feet, a deeply moving encounter.

Have you ever let yourself be cared for as Florence did? Would you be able to cast aside your pride by letting others do for you what you cannot do for yourself? Florence taught me that there is great dignity and honor in being lowly.

Lord, make me lowly in spirit.

AUGUST 17

*For we are the aroma of Christ for God among those who are
being saved and among those who are perishing.*
2 Corinthians 2:15

Meekness is not weakness. In fact, when we embody this
fruit of the Holy Spirit, we communicate a quiet serenity and strength of character. This stands out in contrast
to those who lack control or custody of their emotions. St.
Francis de Sales said that "Nothing is so edifying as charita-
ble meekness. Like oil in a lamp, it keeps the flame of good
example burning."[29]

Living meekly is a worthy goal, a foundation for virtuous
living and for loving others. It is the aroma of Christ in this
world, a fragrance we carry as we honor him and bless others.

Lord, make me meek.

AUGUST 18

See, upon the palms of my hands I have engraved you;
your walls are ever before me.
Isaiah 49:16

Today's verse says that we are engraved on the palms of God's hands; this means we are forever in his grip. It's OK to let ourselves be held. We can ignore but cannot escape his loving embrace! His care is everlasting. He sees the walls—the walls that keep us from receiving his peace, the walls that keep us imprisoned in our fears. These are the walls he will take down, brick by brick, with his love. But for today, let's just rest in him.

Lord, hold me.

AUGUST 19

On the day I cried out, you answered;
you strengthened my spirit.
Psalm 138:3

We all need to be encouraged and strengthened in our spirits from time to time. We get tired, weary, discouraged, grieved, and distraught. Sometimes God sends others to us—earthly angels—to minister with kind words or deeds. Other times we can go to Holy Communion and be filled with consolation and an abiding peace. Sometimes we are strengthened through a waiting period that teaches us patience, endurance, or trust. Whenever we cry out, God will answer us in the way that will best meet our needs. How does your spirit need to be strengthened today?

Lord, strengthen me.

AUGUST 20

Fear of others becomes a snare,
but the one who trusts in the LORD is safe.
Proverbs 29:25

One woman cried out, "I just want to feel safe in my own skin!" She was wearing herself out trying to be what others expected because she was afraid to be her true self. She feared that others would ridicule and reject her. Yet as today's verse says, trust in the Lord is what keeps us safe.

The foundation of every relationship is trust. Discovering and experiencing the Lord's trustworthiness enable us to accept ourselves as we are and feel safe enough to trust others. We grow in trusting people by getting to know them. How will you get to know Jesus better?

Lord, help me to grow in trust.

AUGUST 21

No foul language should come out of your mouths, . . . that [your words] may impart grace to those who hear.
Ephesians 4:29

Tom's workplace was highly competitive, and his boss played favorites, pitting coworkers against one another. Consequently, Tom struggled with stress-related illnesses. Not able to leave the job, he turned to his spiritual director for help.

The wise director suggested that Tom try an experiment by applying today's biblical passage to his situation. He encouraged Tom to conduct a campaign of affirmation and appreciation of his coworkers for the next month. Tom was skeptical, but he agreed to give it a try.

He began by sincerely complimenting some of his most difficult coworkers. He intentionally asked the opinions of those he used to avoid, and he encouraged his archrivals. Halfway through the month, Tom noticed that he no longer dreaded going to work. Instead, he experienced a genuine sense of satisfaction from helping others to feel good about themselves.

Lord, give me the grace to build others up, even those who tear me down.

AUGUST 22

"Your Father knows what you need before you ask him."
Matthew 6:8

What a comfort it is to accept the fact that God knows our needs! There are times when we are too overwhelmed by the circumstances of life to know how to begin to pray. But prayer is not about our words; it's about our hearts. Whether we cry out or remain silent, God will hear us. Our communication with him is not dependent on flowery phrases or perfect recitations.

The psalmist said, "Let my prayer be incense before you; / my uplifted hands an evening offering" (Psalm 141:2). This is a beautiful image of our prayers rising to God, regardless of our words.

Lord, hear me.

AUGUST 23

"Do you want to be well?"
John 5:6

Jesus asked the man who had been lying sick for thirty-eight years at the pool of Bethesda if he wanted to be well, but he knew what the man's answer would be. He asked the question so that the man could give voice to his desire to be made whole. The man didn't answer directly; instead, he gave an explanation. And yet Jesus healed him.

Jesus asks us similar questions. Do you want to overcome your anxiety? Do you want to be free from fear? Do you want to be healed from bitterness, shame, or habitual sin? Whatever ails you, you are invited to proclaim your desire to be made well. When Jesus asks the question, what will your answer be?

Jesus, make me whole.

AUGUST 24

"Whoever follows me will not walk in darkness, but will have the light of life."
John 8:12

"**L**ord, help!" is the most effective prayer I know. For years, I visited a beautiful basilica before work each morning and knelt beneath a life-size crucifix. Most days, I was so riddled with anxiety that I could only muster those two words. But I would look up, and there I'd be, at the feet of Jesus. So lifelike was the wooden crucifix that there was even dirt on Jesus' feet. I would gently touch them and ask to be washed clean of my fears.

I look back now and see how the Lord helped me get through those days. I can retrace my steps and know that he was carrying me. Yet during those years, I didn't know for sure. This is how we walk our own Via Dolorosa. We put one foot in front of the other and cling to the hope of new life, walking out of the darkness with Jesus, one step at a time.

Lord, help!

AUGUST 25

*Fear of the L*ORD *is the beginning of knowledge.*
Proverbs 1:7

Fear of the Lord is a gift of the Holy Spirit. It instills in us a proper honor, reverence, and respect for the sovereignty of God. It puts us in right relationship with him and, in doing so, helps to bring order to all our other relationships and attachments. It's a healthy fear that fills us with a desire to please and not offend God.

We are happiest and most at peace when we serve God, whether we know it or not. Our hearts were made to obey and abide in him. Fear of the Lord means that we treasure that closeness with him. Because we don't want to lose it, we'll do anything to preserve it, including making right choices in life. All of this leads to wisdom and a deep sense of security in knowing who God is and who we are in him.

Lord, fill me with a loving fear of you.

AUGUST 26

But the meek will inherit the land
and enjoy peace and prosperity.
Psalm 37:11 (NIV)

Jesus said it, so it must be true: the meek will inherit the earth and enjoy peace and prosperity. This is the scriptural version of "nice guys finish first." Scripture tells us that at the end of time, there will be "a new heaven and a new earth" (Revelation 21:1). We will not recognize it as the earth that we now know. It will be far better than we can imagine.

Our time here is just a blip on the screen of eternity—and eternity is when the meek will reign. Meekness is worth pursuing because forever is a very long time! And ultimately, that is when we will enjoy the gifts of peace and prosperity.

Lord, I claim my inheritance.

AUGUST 27

FEAST OF ST. MONICA

The fervent prayer of a righteous person is very powerful.

James 5:16

St. Monica had a tough life, but she persevered. She was a long-suffering prayer warrior on behalf of her pagan husband and their wayward son, Augustine. Augustine eventually became one of the greatest saints of all time and a Doctor of the Church, but before his conversion, he was quite a handful. He had a mistress, they had a son, and he refused to accept Christianity in spite of Monica's prayers and entreaties. He caused her great heartache. Monica herself had been a lover of wine as a young woman, but she renounced it when a maid accused her of being a "wine-bibber." She is the patron saint of alcoholics.

Many of us can relate to the messy and imperfect family life that St. Monica experienced. Things were chaotic and far from perfect for most of her life, but the one constant was her ability to pray. No one could take that away from her. Prayer was her anchor and her lifeline. It can be yours as well.

St. Monica, pray for us.

AUGUST 28

But God proves his love for us in that while we were still sinners Christ died for us.

Romans 5:8

St. Augustine of Hippo was smart, handsome, and well aware of his intellectual gifts. He was also addicted to pleasure, as he says in his autobiography *The Confessions,* and had a child with his mistress. On his conversion, he broke off the relationship with his mistress before eventually becoming a priest. His contributions to Christian theology and his influence on Western civilization have been profound. Although St. Augustine knew that he was gifted, he also knew that he was a sinner.

All of Augustine's accomplishments pale in comparison to his personal relationship with Jesus. As he wrote in *The Confessions,* "Our hearts are restless until they rest in you, O Lord." Nothing could fill him up or complete him except the Lord.

If you are praying for someone who is far away from the Lord, pray to St. Augustine. He will be a partner in grace to bring a lost soul home.

St. Augustine, pray for us.

AUGUST 29

*This God who girded me with might, / kept my way
unerring.*
Psalm 18:33

God is our master GPS when we lose our way. On this journey of life, it's easy to take a wrong turn, get distracted, or lose our momentum. We need good directions to navigate through the obstacles and roadblocks along our way. There is a saying that God writes straight in crooked lines. Rerouting is God's specialty. Your path may not always be smooth or straight, but with God as your navigator, you will find your way to your goal.

Lord, lead the way.

AUGUST 30

Offer your bodies as a living sacrifice.
Romans 12:1

A life lived for Christ will always require sacrifice. We'll have to give up people, places, and things that get in the way of serving and loving him with all our hearts, souls, minds, and strength. Starting out small with little sacrifices helps to build up strength to handle bigger sacrifices when the time comes. Foregoing that second cup of coffee, for example, or giving up a comfortable seat to someone else—these little daily denials are not lost on the Lord.

When we practice sacrificial acts of love, we turn away from our own worries and preoccupations and lift our minds to Jesus. He made the ultimate sacrifice. Look for ways to offer yourself today.

Lord, I offer myself to you.

AUGUST 31

"For everyone who asks, receives; and the one who seeks, finds; and to the one who knocks, the door will be opened."
Matthew 7:8

The spiritual life requires effort on our part. We're not supposed to sit back and let God pursue us, though he does. Nevertheless, when we sense that he is seeking us, we must respond. It's like a dance: God leads, and we follow by putting our faith into practice and our belief into action. Ask, seek, knock. How many times a day are you turning to Christ and seeking a heavenly solution for your earthly problems?

Lord, I look to you.

SEPTEMBER

SEPTEMBER 1

*Faith is confidence in what we hope for and assurance
about what we do not see.*
Hebrews 11:1 (NIV)

A simple quote from Dr. Thomas Fuller, a British physician, rings true: "All things are difficult before they are easy."[30] Think about it: everything we have learned to do, we didn't know how to do when we started. To learn how to walk, we had to fall countless times; to learn how to read, we had to memorize an alphabet and figure out how letters come together to form words on a page; to learn how to play an instrument or master a sport, we had to perfect our technique. To stay the course, though, in every instance, we had to have faith in ourselves, believing that we would eventually succeed.

We can apply faith to any challenge that confronts us. We receive the gift of this virtue in Baptism. The difficulties along life's journey can't undermine our faith unless we make the choice to let them.

Lord, thank you for the gift of faith.

SEPTEMBER 2

"I do believe, help my unbelief!"
Mark 9:24

It's amazing that when Jesus performed miracle upon miracle, even raising people from the dead, the people who should have known him best refused to accept him. He spoke with authority as the Son of God, but few believed him. Instead, they were limited by their narrow view of who they *thought* he was or who they expected him to be. They only saw the carpenter's son. Jesus himself lamented, "No prophet is accepted in his own native place" (Luke 4:24). The biases of the people limited what he was able to do among them.

How many times have you said to yourself, "I can't change, so why should I bother trying?" We assume that we have exhausted all possibilities, but God has an infinite arsenal of grace to aid us in our personal transformation. In the "native place" of your own mind, don't limit what God can do to help you change your present circumstance or heal your brokenness. He is who he says he is. Believe and be ready to see him anew.

Lord, give me eyes to see you and an open heart that will help me change for the better.

SEPTEMBER 3

He was amazed at their lack of faith.
Mark 6:6

If faith is a gift, then why do so many of those who are baptized seem to lack it? The *Catechism* offers an explanation:

> To be human, "man's response to God by faith must be free, and . . . therefore nobody is to be forced to embrace the faith against his will. The act of faith is of its very nature a free act." "God calls men to serve him in spirit and in truth. Consequently they are bound to him in conscience, but not coerced." (160)

> We can lose this priceless gift. . . . To live, grow, and persevere in the faith until the end we must nourish it with the word of God; we must beg the Lord to increase our faith. (162)

Let's not let a lack of faith limit what Jesus can do in our lives. When we pray, let's put faith at the top of the list so that Jesus is free to perform miracles in our midst.

Lord, increase my faith.

SEPTEMBER 4

I am confident of this, that the one who began a good work in you will continue to complete it until the day of Christ Jesus.

Philippians 1:6

I keep starting over. I suppose that's better than the alternative—being at the end with no more chances. It seems as if the Lord always wants me to be at the beginning of something new. What better way to remind me that I am not the expert! In fact, just when I think I have things figured out, he changes it up, and I am a beginner again, stretching and growing.

Pope Benedict XVI said, "Man was created for greatness— for God himself; he was created to be filled by God. But his heart is too small for the greatness to which it is destined. It must be stretched."[31]

So, with greatness as our aim, it stands to reason that we will never be finished in this lifetime. We will forever need to start anew, over and over, until we are completed, by grace, in God.

Lord, let every step be a step toward your perfect will for me.

SEPTEMBER 5

"The LORD will fight for you; you have only to keep still."
Exodus 14:14

So how can you be still? One way is to resist the temptation to formulate a solution to every problem or control the outcomes of your interactions with others. Let the Holy Spirit breathe life into difficult situations; let the Lord do what he does best.

Another way to be still is to abide. When we abide in something, we remain, wait, or dwell in it. Jesus entreated us to abide in him, and he gave a good visual of how to do that. He said, "I am the vine, you are the branches. Whoever remains in me and I in him will bear much fruit, because without me you can do nothing" (John 15:5).

Branches are utterly dependent on the vine to grow and bear fruit. A good deal of our anxiety can stem from the belief that we alone must produce the fruit. When we feel this internal pressure, let's remember that God calls us to be still and trust him to do the rest.

Lord, I abide in you.

SEPTEMBER 6

Jesus said . . . , "Unless you people see signs and wonders,
you will not believe."
John 4:48

Miracles are unfolding every day, but we may not be aware of them. When we are praying hard for something, we usually have an idea in mind about the outcome we'd like to see. We may offer more than a gentle suggestion to God about how he should proceed. Thankfully he is a patient God who understands our tendency to step in and tell him how to get things done.

Don't focus so hard on your own desired outcome that you miss the miracle in the making that God is unfolding before you. Maybe this is why God gives us rainbows, so that we will look up and realize he is still on the job. It's his promise to us that miracles are happening all the time; we just need to look for them.

Lord, help me to be open to all your possible
answers to my prayers.

SEPTEMBER 7

For we walk by faith, not by sight.
2 Corinthians 5:7

We can't always protect our children, but we can pre-pare them. We can teach them, but we cannot tether them. Just as they will need to take a leap of faith to grow and become who God calls them to be, we will have to take that same leap to let them go.

Trying to shield our children from disappointments or mistakes does more to cripple them than to console them. They will grow in confidence through their failures, perhaps more than through their successes. This is part of maturing in the walk of faith. Your children's journeys will not look like your own. Release them to discover what they believe, trusting that Jesus is with them and hears your prayers.

Jesus, help my children walk by faith.

SEPTEMBER 8

THE NATIVITY OF THE BLESSED VIRGIN MARY
"Behold, I am the handmaid of the Lord."
Luke 1:38

We celebrate Marian feasts because we want to honor Mary. She's with us every day, interceding on our behalf behind the scenes. Today we observe her birthday. How will you celebrate with Mary?

Like most mothers, she doesn't draw attention to herself and is happiest when her children are happy. Can you share your joy with her today? Let her know how much you delight in her Son. Take a joy break with her, and count your blessings. The best gift you can give her is you.

Happy Birthday, Blessed Mother!

SEPTEMBER 9

Hence, now there is no condemnation for those who are in Christ Jesus.
Romans 8:1

Anxiety is often fueled by a compulsive need to know what other people are thinking or doing. Somehow, this kind of knowledge helps us feel OK. But when we live in this defensive way, we give away our personal power. We become suspicious and perpetually on guard, trying to figure others out so that they will accept us.

Let this sink in: there is no condemnation in Christ Jesus. His is the only opinion that matters. We don't have to measure up to the standards of others, control what they think, or try to anticipate what they want. We are free to focus on Jesus and his accepting, unconditional love for us. There is nothing we can do or say that can diminish our worth in his eyes. He forever beholds us as precious and dear.

Lord, thank you for loving me.

SEPTEMBER 10

"Whoever believes in me, as scripture says:
'Rivers of living water will flow from within him.'"
John 7:38

Have you ever been completely depleted of good ideas, inspiration, creativity, or energy? Those who suffer depression sometimes say that when the depression hits, they experience not so much a feeling of sadness as a pervasive inner emptiness or numbness. Whether through depression or because of other circumstances, we all experience these desert times to some degree. Jesus himself went out into the desert. He experienced barrenness, hunger, and temptation, just as we do.

During desert times, we need to hold on to our faith, no matter how we feel inside. Jesus promises to provide us with what we need to keep going. His "rivers of living waters" carry with them the graces, spiritual refreshment, and fortification we need. When we have nothing left to give, Jesus gives us everything he has to get us through.

Lord, fill me.

SEPTEMBER 11

Put on the armor of God so that you may be able to stand
firm against the tactics of the devil.
Ephesians 6:11

Joan of Arc said, "All battles are first won or lost, in the
mind."[32] Let today be the day that you declare a cease-fire
for the thoughts that, like missiles, defeat and deflate you.
Replace them with a vision of victory over your worries and
fears. The full armor of God looks like this:

> Your loins girded in truth, clothed with righteousness as
> a breastplate, and your feet shod in readiness for the gos-
> pel of peace. In all circumstances, hold faith as a shield,
> to quench all [the] flaming arrows of the evil one. And
> take the helmet of salvation and the sword of the Spirit,
> which is the word of God. (Ephesians 6:14-17)

You can lead the charge for peace on the battlefield of
your mind.

Lord, hear my battle cry!

SEPTEMBER 12

"Nothing will be impossible for you."
Matthew 17:20

There seems to be a great deal of untapped faith among the followers of Jesus across the ages. He even addressed this issue with his disciples when they asked him why they could not drive out a particularly pesky demon. He replied,

"Because of your little faith. Amen, I say to you, if you have faith the size of a mustard seed, you will say to this mountain, 'Move from here to there,' and it will move. Nothing will be impossible for you." (Matthew 17:20)

Faith is not magic, but as the *Catechism* says, "Faith is *certain*. It is more certain than all human knowledge because it is founded on the very word of God who cannot lie" (157).

Jesus said that "nothing will be impossible for you." Do you believe him?

Lord, increase my faith.

SEPTEMBER 13

*L*ORD, *you are our father; / we are the clay and you our pot-*
ter: / we are all the work of your hand.
Isaiah 64:7

Pressure in the proper measure is a good thing. Under pressure, for example, a lump of coal becomes a diamond, and
a hunk of clay becomes a piece of porcelain. Similarly, we need
to feel a certain amount of pressure in order to reach our full
potential. So, at the first sign of pressure, don't panic. Stop,
take a breath, and consider how to respond to the pressure
so that your best self emerges in any situation.

If it gets to be too much for you, back away for a bit. The
resting periods in any great project are just as important as the
times of productivity. Let the Master work with you to bring
about the beautiful masterpiece he wants to make of your life.

Lord, shape me.

SEPTEMBER 14

FEAST OF THE EXALTATION OF THE CROSS
He humbled himself, / becoming obedient to death, / even death on a cross. / Because of this, God greatly exalted him.
Philippians 2:8-9

The feast of the Exaltation of the Holy Cross is a powerful one for people who are anxious and overwhelmed. It marks the victory that Christ won for us through his passion and death: namely, freedom from sin and all that keeps us in bondage.

Following Jesus will lead us out of our misery and prison of self. We can't follow him and stay stuck in our fear. Some days, I envision carrying the cross labeled anxiety alongside Jesus, and I simply exchange my cross with his.

St. John of the Cross said that "the endurance of darkness is preparation for great light."[33] There was no darker day then the day Jesus was crucified, but now his cross is a sign of hope and triumph. Claim your victory in him today.

Lord, by your cross you set us free.

SEPTEMBER 15

FEAST OF OUR LADY OF SORROWS

And from that hour the disciple took her into his home.
John 19:27

Mary is a mother who knows our pain. Maybe that is why Jesus, on the cross, shared her in a special way when he said to the beloved disciple—and by extension to all of us— "Behold, your mother" (John 19:27). Mary's role in the Church and in our lives is focused on keeping us close to Jesus. She is always right there with him, drawing people closer to his heart. For those who are concerned about Mary's role, St. Maximilian Kolbe said, "Never be afraid of loving the Blessed Virgin too much. You can never love her more than Jesus did."[34]

Invite Mary into your home, your life, and your heart. She wants to be in solidarity with you in your sufferings and celebrations, sharing tears of sorrow and of joy alike.

Dear Mother Mary, come be with me.

SEPTEMBER 16

I have set my face like flint, / knowing that I shall not
be put to shame.
Isaiah 50:7

Flint is a very hard rock, used to create sparks and in ancient times for making tools and weapons. If we are said to be "like flint," we are standing firm, remaining committed, strong in our convictions, and determined. Today's verse captures the sense of power we have when we refuse to carry the burden of shame.

Shame is a strong emotion, but it's not the truth of who we are. Rather than saying we did something bad or made a mistake, we internalize a message that says, "I *am* something bad." Allowing shame to define us can restrict our openness to God's healing love, leading to depression or despair. The Scriptures say that Jesus came to "let the oppressed go free" (Luke 4:18). That includes freedom from toxic shame and self-loathing.

Lord, I resist destructive shame.

SEPTEMBER 17

Christ lives in me; insofar as I now live in the flesh, I live
by faith in the Son of God who has loved me and given
himself up for me.
Galatians 2:20

We can either live by faith or live by fear. Whatever we feed—faith or fear—that's what will grow within us. If Christ lives in us, then there will be little room for fear. He will plant the gifts of the Holy Spirit within us: wisdom, understanding, counsel, fortitude, knowledge, piety, and fear of the Lord. He will tend these gifts day by day, nurturing them by his love. We can freely choose what we plant and allow to flourish in our hearts.

Feed your faith, not your fears.

Lord, I choose faith.

SEPTEMBER 18

*I continue my pursuit toward the goal, the prize of God's
upward calling, in Christ Jesus.*
Philippians 3:14

A s far as our spiritual lives are concerned, we are not in
a sprint but a marathon. We need perseverance and
endurance to get to our destination—we have to be in it for
the long haul. Don't be in too much of a hurry to run your
race. We are all going to get to the finish line at the time God
chooses. Our job is to run well, applying the best strategies
that will ensure we can go the distance. Let's set a reasonable
pace that keeps us focused but not out of breath.

Lord, keep me on track.

SEPTEMBER 19

"Whatever you ask for in prayer with faith,
you will receive."
Matthew 21:22

When I was ten years old, my aunt was diagnosed with liver and lung cancer. She was mother to five children under the age of fifteen—it was devastating news. Most people didn't survive a cancer diagnosis back then, and she didn't either. Despite all my prayers and promises to my cousins that God would answer us and heal her, he didn't. They were mad at God and heartbroken, as was the whole family.

I can tell you that her death wasn't due to a lack of faith—I truly believed that God would heal her. When he didn't, I had a choice to make. I was only ten, but I decided to trust God anyway. I believe that my aunt today is living in his heavenly embrace or at least on her way there. Someday, I hope to know exactly how God answered that prayer.

Lord, I trust you.

SEPTEMBER 20

For one believes with the heart and so is justified, and one confesses with the mouth and so is saved.

Romans 10:10

Today's verse extols the value of walking the walk and talking the talk as a follower of Jesus. What we do and say matters. When our words and actions are in harmony with one another, we are true witnesses to the hope that is in Christ Jesus.

We need grace upon grace to be morally coherent and single-hearted—it isn't always easy. We need the sacraments and the supernatural strength that comes from them. We are able to carry out our good works through the life and light of our Catholic faith and our life in the Church. We are blessed to have Jesus in our midst. Go to him and be justified and saved.

Lord, receive me.

SEPTEMBER 21

And the apostles said to the Lord, "Increase our faith."
Luke 17:5

Throughout most of Jesus' public ministry, his apostles were utterly clueless about what was going on. Even though these twelve were the closest to him of all his followers, they stumbled and fumbled around in their misunderstanding. Yet still they followed him. In the midst of all of their questions, they were smart enough to ask for one important thing: an increase in faith.

You can't go wrong if you follow suit. Jesus is going to answer any heartfelt prayer to increase faith. Like the apostles, you may need to fall a few times and make some mistakes along the way, but when you ask for an increase in faith, Jesus finds your prayer irresistible. Look what he did for the twelve apostles! He can do the same for us.

Lord, increase my faith.

SEPTEMBER 22

*Let us no longer judge one another, but rather resolve never
to put a stumbling block or hindrance in the
way of a brother.*
Romans 14:13

St. Paul's letter to the growing Christian community in Rome seems especially pertinent today. The Romans were arguing over which religious practices were acceptable, and they were judging others for being too stringent in their faith or not devout enough. Sound familiar?

Wouldn't it be wonderful if we resolved never to put a stumbling block in front of someone who was honestly trying to practice the faith, even if their approach differed from ours? If they were getting offtrack, we'd address that, of course, but we'd do so kindly and respectfully, in a spirit of encouragement and hospitality.

Lord, help me to be a help and not a hindrance.

SEPTEMBER 23

"Can any of you by worrying add a single moment to your
life-span?"
Matthew 6:27

Today is the feast day of St. Padre Pio, who said most mem-
orably, "Pray, hope, and don't worry." I don't know about
you, but I never appreciate it when some well-meaning person
tells me not to worry when I'm having a panic attack or facing
an overwhelming circumstance. Of course I wouldn't worry if
I could stop myself, but sometimes it doesn't feel like a choice.

Padre Pio's statement reminds us, though, that worry can't
be our *only* response to troubling situations. We have the option
of adding prayer and hope to the mix, thus putting things in
the right order.

We pray first, and then we activate hope. We can stir up hope
by remembering the ways that Jesus has gotten us through
past worrisome episodes, trusting that he will do so again. Let
hope trump worry through the intercession of St. Pio today.

St. Padre Pio, help me cope with hope.

SEPTEMBER 24

"Lord, I am not worthy . . ."
Matthew 8:8

Every week at Mass we repeat the words of the centurion in today's verse: "Lord, I am not worthy that you should enter under my roof, but only say the word and my soul shall be healed." Scripture says that Jesus was "amazed" by these words and the faith of the man who uttered them. The centurion knew in his heart that Jesus could heal his servant without even going to see him. He understood the authority Jesus had both in heaven and on earth, and he respected it. In turn, Jesus rewarded the centurion richly.

Don't you want to amaze Jesus with your faith too?

Lord, heal my soul.

SEPTEMBER 25

*That he may grant you in accord with the riches of his glory
to be strengthened with power through his Spirit in the inner
self, and that Christ may dwell in your hearts through faith.*
Ephesians 3:16-17

"Go to the throne instead of the phone." This pithy saying takes on new meaning in this era of rapidly changing technology when so many of us struggle with feeling tethered to our phones. With the world at our fingertips, faith can take a backseat. We can pull out our phone and instantly look up any answer to any question, but we won't find God's answers on our phones. He speaks to us and answers our questions in the depths of our hearts.

Lord, I seek your answers within.

SEPTEMBER 26

"You are the salt of the earth. But if salt loses its taste,
with what can it be seasoned?"
Matthew 5:13

I remember the day I became a good cook. It's the day I stopped trying to follow a recipe to a T and began experimenting with my own ideas. Reflecting on it now, it has been a metaphor for my life. Every time I have tried to fit perfectly into a role I felt I was supposed to play, I lost an essential ingredient . . . me!

Following Jesus doesn't mean that we become a cookie-cutter Christian who looks, sounds, and thinks like everybody else. He doesn't want us to lose our personalities. In fact, just the opposite: we are called to be unique, individual expressions of God's image on earth, bringing our own brand of saltiness to the table so that all can "taste and see" the goodness of the Lord (see Psalm 34:9).

Lord, thank you for making me . . . me.

SEPTEMBER 27

*"Your light must shine before others, that they may see your
good deeds and glorify your heavenly Father."*
Matthew 5:16

Jesus doesn't give us a choice: he says our light *must* shine!
No putting it under a bushel basket, no hiding in the shadows, no false humility keeping us from sharing his light in us.
What good deeds has God called you to do? If you're not sure,
ask the Holy Spirit to reveal them to you. Fulfilling your purpose so that God gets the glory will settle your soul and fill you
with peace. Step out of the darkness and shine.

Lord, be glorified.

SEPTEMBER 28

"I, the LORD, explore the mind / and test the heart, / Giving to all according to their ways, / according to the fruit of their deeds."
Jeremiah 17:10

Resist the temptation to think of anxiety as a huge, foreboding black cloud that overtakes you. Anxiety can manifest itself on a continuum from mild concern to full-blown panic, but how we experience it and label it will give us some control over how we respond to it. Instead of overreacting or underreacting, put your anxious feelings on the continuum. Are you mildly worried, deeply concerned, excited, nervous, or some other level in between the extremes?

Ask the Lord to search and test the level of your anxiety with you. Get *his* perspective so that you can root out any distortion that might affect your ability to see things correctly. His light will give you the perfect view.

Lord, search me.

SEPTEMBER 29

The Feast of the Archangels
Bless the Lord, all you his angels, / mighty in strength, acting at his behest, / obedient to his command.
Psalm 103:20

The Bible mentions three archangels by name, each with specific functions: Michael is a warrior, Gabriel is a messenger, and Raphael is a healer. It's comforting to know that we *always* have angels with us. Our guardian angels are always at our side, of course, but when we need an extra boost, we can call on an archangel.

We are probably most familiar with Michael, who thrust Satan into hell and works overtime to keep wayward souls from evil. Gabriel appeared to Zechariah and Mary to speak to them respectively of the conception of John the Baptist and Jesus. We read of Raphael, whose name means "God heals," in the Book of Tobit, which describes how he healed Tobit of blindness and freed Tobit's future daughter-in-law from a demon.

We are in good company when we are in the company of angels. Which archangel do you need in your life today?

Lord, I treasure your angels of light.

SEPTEMBER 30

I will turn their mourning into joy,
I will show them compassion and have them rejoice after
their sorrows.
Jeremiah 31:13

We will all experience sorrow, but it is just as certain that we will experience joy—God says we will. He will turn our sadness into gladness. Let us not resist this!

One woman said, "I am afraid to be happy because I'm always waiting for the other shoe to drop." Instead of expecting something good to happen, she was pouring her energy into fearing the worst.

Let's flip the switch. When we are going through a difficult or dark time, let the light of God's promise shine through. Anticipate joy. It will come.

Lord, gladden my heart.

OCTOBER

OCTOBER 1

*"Whoever receives one child such as this in my name,
receives me; and whoever receives me, receives not me
but the One who sent me."*

Mark 9:37

Today is the memorial of St. Thérèse of Lisieux, a Doctor of the Church who championed a "little way" of spirituality open to all. As a child, Thérèse dealt with tremendous grief over several significant losses, including the death of her mother. As a result, she had an extremely sensitive temperament. Today, she might well be diagnosed as suffering from attachment disorder or separation anxiety.

Thérèse's wounds and challenges didn't discourage her in her desire to become a saint, however. She knew she wasn't capable of lofty things, so she strove to make love her sole vocation. She took to heart our Lord's invitation to approach him as a child in purity and simplicity, trusting him to help her grow in holiness. He did!

Dear Father God, I'm grateful to be your child.

OCTOBER 2

No evil shall befall you, / no affliction come near your tent. / For he commands his angels with regard to you, / to guard you wherever you go.

Psalm 91:10-11

Our guardian angels serve us by helping us turn away from evil and temptation. According to the *Catechism,* "Beside each believer stands an angel as protector and shepherd leading him to life" (336). What a comfort it is to know that we have such faithful friends in high places!

We can call upon other people's guardian angels in prayer as well. If you're concerned about someone, you can ask your guardian angel to unite with theirs in a spiritual tag team of special protection. Our heavenly protectors always have our back.

Angel of God, my guardian dear, watch over me and always be near; guide my steps, wherever I go, and protect me from the snares below.

OCTOBER 3

[Jesus] said, "Come." Peter got out of the boat and began to walk on the water toward Jesus.
Matthew 14:29

Good old St. Peter! He seemed to have a thing for jumping out of a boat. Whether with a sense of purpose or reckless abandon, Peter never shied away from stepping out of his comfort zone. He jumped into the deep waters of his life. Regardless of the consequences, Peter persevered, even trying to do the impossible by walking on water to Jesus.

Peter's exuberance teaches us an important lesson: we don't have to be afraid to fail. Our friend Peter often did, but he never let those failings get in the way of receiving Jesus' restoring love. Peter was headstrong, but he was also humble because he wasn't afraid to reveal his shortcomings. He didn't try to hide his imperfections from Jesus. Instead, he said, "Depart from me, Lord, for I am a sinful man" (Luke 5:8).

Jump in. Jesus is waiting!

Lord, I'm coming.

OCTOBER 4

I will listen for what God, the LORD, has to say.
Psalm 85:9

W e've all experienced being "talked at" by someone intent on getting a point across. We sit there and try to take it in, but after a while, our eyes glaze over and our minds wander as we disengage from the one-sided conversation. Thankfully God doesn't do that. He's always listening.

Listening to others is a highly effective way for us to grow in humility—it demands that we pay attention. But listening has a place in prayer as well. During prayer time, intentionally set aside a few minutes to sit quietly and listen to the Lord. You might consider the practice of *lectio divina*, or "divine reading." Essentially, *lectio* involves reading a short Scripture passage slowly several times, pausing in between to reflect on what the Holy Spirit is saying specifically to you through the text. A word or idea may strike you; if so, you ponder what it means and how you can apply it to your life. *Lectio divina* becomes an intimate dialogue with God, a beautiful way to listen to what he has to say to you.

Lord, speak to me.

OCTOBER 5

*So humble yourselves under the mighty hand of God, that he
may exalt you in due time.*
1 Peter 5:6

St. John Bosco said, "Humility is the source of all peace."[35] It's a bold statement but entirely true when you discover that humility isn't thinking less of yourself; it's thinking of yourself less. Our preoccupations, self-consciousness, and worries about how we are being perceived give way to a deep abiding peace through the virtue of humility.

Humility doesn't mean that we neglect ourselves or our needs. Instead, as we grow in humility, we become free from the desire to be important or be acknowledged for the things we do. A greater desire burns within us to remain hidden, giving our Lord all the glory. A humble person is rarely offended, taking criticism and humiliations in stride. In practicing humility, we have nothing to prove and great inner freedom to gain.

Lord, I seek humility and peace.

OCTOBER 6

Cast all your worries upon him because he cares for you.
1 Peter 5:7

As we walk through life, we collect heavy burdens. Some of them we can't avoid, and some of them we can, but we can cast all of them upon the Lord. That's a cause for joy. We serve an awesome God who not only created the universe, but also cares for each one of us individually. He will never turn his back on us or say, *"Enough,* I'm done!"

We don't have to hold back our needs from the Lord. His care covers all. In fact, he told St. Faustina,

> I am love and Mercy Itself. There is no misery that could be a match for My mercy, neither will misery exhaust it, because as it is being granted—it increases. The soul that trusts in My mercy is most fortunate, because I Myself take care of it.[36]

Lord, thank you for caring for me.

OCTOBER 7

OUR LADY OF THE ROSARY
"Hail, favored one."
Luke 1:28

During the month of October, we honor Mary as Our Lady of the Rosary. Fulton Sheen said that "the power of the rosary is beyond description."[37] Not only that, but the rhythmic and repetitive prayers are soothing, and the meditations draw us into the life of Jesus. For anyone struggling with anxiety, the Rosary can be a lifeline.

We are encouraged to pray the Rosary every day, but don't get scrupulous about it. That would defeat the purpose. Be consoled by the fact that St. Thérèse struggled to pray it, saying,

> In vain do I strive to meditate on the mysteries of the Rosary; I am unable to fix my attention. For a long time I was sad because of this lack of devotion . . . now it saddens me less; I think that the Queen of Heaven being my Mother, she must see my good will and be content with it.[38]

The Rosary is a gift from Mary. Our recitation of it is our gift to her.

Mother of God, pray for us.

OCTOBER 8

*Clothe yourselves with humility in your dealings with one
another, for: / "God opposes the proud /
but bestows favor on the humble."*
1 Peter 5:5

Every day we put at least a few minutes into thinking about
the clothes we'll wear that day and how we'll present ourselves to the world. Whether it is manic Monday or casual Friday,
our clothes need to match the conditions and responsibilities
of the day. Something similar happens when we clothe ourselves in virtue—sometimes we'll need one virtue more than
another—but putting on humility is never optional. It is essential gear for any and every kind of weather.

Humility never goes out of fashion, and it's attractive, especially to God. Those who wear humility, day in and day out, find
favor with him. I want to be one of those people, don't you?

Lord, help me wear humility well.

OCTOBER 9

We look not to what is seen but to what is unseen; for what is seen is transitory, but what is unseen is eternal.
2 Corinthians 4:18

You can't surrender what you won't acknowledge. In other words, when we ignore our fears, they can keep us tethered to the very things we are afraid of. It can take a long time to let go of our fears because we may not know who we are without them. In fact, they may even be part of how we define ourselves.

Surrender is not a one-time act. It is our daily work. We surrender all the things, seen and unseen, that get in the way of our freedom to walk with Jesus.

Holy Spirit, enlighten me.

OCTOBER 10

He shows pity to the needy and the poor
and saves the lives of the poor.
Psalm 72:13

We are all poor in different ways. Our hearts are restless, we need more virtue, we lack answers to many of life's questions, and we may be struggling with material poverty. Yet still our Lord loves us. He says, "Blessed are the poor in spirit, / for theirs is the kingdom of heaven" (Matthew 5:3).

Being poor in spirit means that we acknowledge our limitations and seek first the things of God. We don't have to try to be something or someone we are not. We trust in God more than in ourselves.

Anxiety can stem from a denial of our poverty and our need for a savior. Rejoice in your poverty today so that you can experience all the goodness of God's kingdom here on earth.

Lord, save me.

OCTOBER 11

Do nothing out of selfishness or out of vainglory; rather, humbly regard others as more important than yourselves.
Philippians 2:3

Imagine what it would be like if you and everyone you met in the next week followed the instruction in today's verse. Your corner of the world could be completely changed if you adopted this prescription for humility.

Much of our unhappiness and strife come from an inordinate need to be noticed and an attachment to the accolades of others. The *Catechism* says that baptized people should train themselves in humility. It goes on to quote St. John Chrysostom, who said, "Would you like to see God glorified by you? Then rejoice in your brother's progress and you will immediately give glory to God" (2540).

Humility, when applied, will change our hearts and the world.

Lord, I glorify you.

OCTOBER 12

Whenever the vessel of clay he was making turned out badly
in his hand, he tried again, making another vessel of
whatever sort he pleased.
Jeremiah 18:4

With Jesus, we always get a do-over. If we approach him with a sincere and contrite heart and a firm intention to avoid sin, he forgives us. Once again, we are free to be made new in his image.

The Japanese have a tradition called *kintsugi,* or "golden repair art." They don't discard pottery when it's cracked or broken; instead, they apply a liquid gold inlay to repair it. *Kintsugi* is a metaphor for life, acknowledging that beauty comes out of the brokenness, and "scars" make something unique.

There is a message in *kintsugi* for us: even with our brokenness—our sins and weaknesses—we are valuable to God. Instead of gold inlay, the precious blood of our Lord fills the gap. By his blood, we are healed and made whole.

Lord, repair me.

OCTOBER 13

Do not be conquered by evil but conquer evil with good.
Romans 12:21

The devil is sometimes called the enemy of our souls. It's true that he is our most formidable foe, but he has nothing on God. In the battle between good and evil, love and hate, love always wins.

In an article on the website Those Catholic Men, Fr. Dwight Longenecker writes that the best way to combat evil "is not to pray against the evil directly, but to pray *for* what is positive."[39] In other words, instead of praying for the end of an addiction or against the evil of it, we pray for the addict's restoration in mind, body, and soul, as well as for all those who are supporting him. We pray for the success of the treatment approaches, wisdom for the workers and counselors, and perseverance for all involved.

As Fr. Longenecker concludes, "The best way to counter all that is ugly, evil, and false is to support all that is beautiful, good, and true."

Lord, let your goodness reign.

OCTOBER 14

Be very careful, then, how you live—not as unwise but as wise, making the most of every opportunity.
Ephesians 5:15-16 (NIV)

Overcommitment can be a trap. The world values multitasking, but when we're overextended, stress is sure to follow. This shows up most often in our relationships with those who are closest to us. They get the short end of the stick of frazzled nerves and lack of time and attention.

Saying no can be an act of humility. A simple no testifies to the fact that the world can go on without us. Not every group needs our input; not every project requires our effort. When we dial it back, we may discover that our overcommitting stems more from a need to be liked than from pleasing God.

Here are a few key phrases that can help: "I'm sorry, but I'm not able to help you at this time"; "That sounds interesting, but I have a full schedule right now"; "No" (and that's really a complete sentence!).

Lord, help me to be careful about how I spend my time.

OCTOBER 15

May the God of hope fill you with all joy and peace in believing, so that you may abound in hope by the power of the holy Spirit.
Romans 15:13

St. Teresa of Avila, whose feast is today, said, "You pay God a compliment by asking great things of Him."[40] When was the last time you paid God a compliment? Have you been holding back from big dreams or large-scale requests because you don't want to get your hopes up?

To protect ourselves from disappointment, we can go through life with very low expectations. In doing so, however, we can quench our spirits and even stymie the action of the Holy Spirit. God has a better way.

When we hope in God, we will never be disappointed. His will is the greatest and highest good we can experience here on earth. Asking him for great things and then not getting them only means that we are getting what is best for us right now. God cannot be outdone in his goodness. We need to *aim high* in all that we do and desire. The Holy Spirit will take it from there.

Lord, I am asking you for _____.

OCTOBER 16

"If God is for us, who can be against us?"
Romans 8:31

God's got our back, 24/7. To seal the deal, he has assigned each of us our own personal angel to watch over us, and he's sent his Holy Spirit to be our Advocate, Comforter, Counselor, and Guide. As children of God and members of a communion of saints that never sleeps, we're covered.

St. Paul offered even greater encouragement when he wrote,

I am convinced that neither death, nor life, nor angels, nor principalities, nor present things, nor future things, nor powers, nor height, nor depth, nor any other creature will be able to separate us from the love of God in Christ Jesus our Lord. (Romans 8:38-39)

God is on our side. With him, we can conquer anything.

Lord, let's roll!

OCTOBER 17

Jesus said . . . , "I am the way and the truth and the life."
John 14:6

My friend Kathy was confronting a difficult family situation. She told me she was trying to yank herself out of the stress and worry lane and get into the slow lane with Jesus. What a great image! What do we do when we change lanes? Slow down, look around, and commit.

In a similar way, when we are changing the pace or direction of our lives, we slow down, look around, and commit. And we keep Jesus firmly in view. He doesn't just know the way—he *is* the way.

Lord, ride with me.

OCTOBER 18

My times are in Your hand;
Deliver me.
Psalm 31:15 (NASB)

According to a popular saying, you can't reach for what is in front of you until you let go of what's behind you. Your past is your past. Take what you need, and leave the rest behind. Some burdens are better cast aside. If you look back, take the gold from your hard-won lessons, not the gravel of your failures. Carry the gold proudly. This is the wisdom, strength, and confidence you have won. Let these bless you as you walk in the knowledge that you have survived.

Even God cannot change your past, but your future is in his hands. Move on.

Lord, deliver me.

OCTOBER 19

God has made everything appropriate to its time, but has put the timeless into their hearts.

Ecclesiastes 3:11

Every day I pull out my grandmother's metal measuring spoons to make my morning coffee. The irony that I am now a grandmother myself is not lost on me. The spoons and I both classify as antiques. Where did the time go?

One thing that anxiety does well is to rob us of enjoying the simple pleasures of life: a good cup of coffee, a warm bath, the sweet memory of baking cookies in your grandmother's kitchen. Don't let anxiety have its day!

The richness and depth of our lives come from the ordinary moments. Cherish them. We live an average of 37,739,520 minutes! Savor every second.

Lord, teach me to number my days.

OCTOBER 20

For I have learned to be content in whatever
circumstances I am.
Philippians 4:11 (NASB)

God's beautiful gift of free will is an important avenue to peace. We always have a choice regarding how we respond to the circumstances of life. We can choose to be offended or merciful; jealous or encouraging; annoyed or detached; overwhelmed or at peace.

Holocaust survivor Viktor Frankl said, "Everything can be taken from a man but one thing: the last of the human freedom—to choose one's attitude in any given set of circumstances."[41]

He survived one of the worst tragedies in human history, but he recognized that it was up to him to determine how he would integrate the experience into his life. We have the same freedom, should we choose to exercise it.

Lord, help me to choose wisely.

OCTOBER 21

Your adornment should not be an external one . . . , but rather the hidden character of the heart, expressed in the imperishable beauty of a gentle and calm disposition.
1 Peter 3:3, 4

If we try to look good on the outside, but neglect our interior well-being, it will catch up with us. The only true, imperishable beauty is that which shines from the inside out as we nurture the hidden person within.

Similarly, it doesn't matter what temperament we may have—if we are an outgoing and gregarious person, or a tried-and-true introvert. What matters is that we connect with God and become settled in our spirits. When we do, we grow in quiet, gentle confidence, knowing we are precious in God's sight.

Lord, shine through me.

OCTOBER 22

Do everything without grumbling or questioning, that you
may be blameless and innocent, children of God without
blemish in the midst of a crooked and perverse generation,
among whom you shine like lights in the world.
Philippians 2:14-15

The instruction in today's verse is a tall order. If I counted every complaint I make during a day, spoken or unspoken, I could probably fill a large bucket. Some versions of the Bible call this murmuring—essentially putting our two cents in when it's not needed.

The Israelites, on the way to the Promised Land, perfected the art of grumbling. Though God provided for their every need, they always found fault; they were never satisfied. Even when he was literally in their midst, they felt abandoned by him. As a result, God allowed what should have been a three-month trip to last for forty years.

The next time you are tempted to grumble about or question what God is doing in your life, think about the Israelites. We can either wander around aimlessly or shine like lights in the world. Which would you prefer?

Lord, help me to shine.

OCTOBER 23

But Moses answered the people, "Do not fear! Stand your ground and see the victory the LORD will win for you today."
Exodus 14:13

Life feels like a battle at times. How often do we expect to see victory in the Lord? We need to anticipate his triumph over our troubles so that we can stand our ground and declare a win over worry and distress. If we are not emerging victorious in our spirits, it might be because we won't get out of his way.

Today's verse says that the Lord will win the battle. So often, we think that we have to go it alone, but we don't. God is our protector, our refuge, and our strength. Let him do what he does. He is God Almighty and is ready to do battle for you today.

Lord, make haste to help me.

OCTOBER 24

Death and life are in the power of the tongue;
those who choose one shall eat its fruit.
Proverbs 18:21

My friend is a half-empty sort of gal. She can put in a full day at work, grocery shop on the way home, set a meal on the table, give her kids a bath, and lament that she didn't get anything done. She's not seeing what she has accomplished, only what she has left to do. Occasionally, I have to remind her to dial back the negativity and tune into the positive frequency of things. It's not her natural inclination, but she can do it with a bit of encouragement.

Psychologists call this "reframing." It's a valuable technique for "altering negative or self-defeating thought patterns by deliberately replacing them with positive, constructive self-talk."[42]

What we say can raise us up or tear us down. We can search for the good or sink in a sea of negativity. Let's work on adopting a positive frame of mind and self-talk that breathes life into our souls and joy into our hearts. We have the power to choose.

Lord, raise me up.

OCTOBER 25

The choicest first fruits of your soil you shall bring to the house of the LORD, your God.

Exodus 34:26

St. Edith Stein, before she became a Carmelite nun, was a successful professional with a myriad of responsibilities and pressures. She understood well the stress of trying to get everything done. Her advice on how to handle it is as relevant today as when she gave it:

> The duties and cares of the day ahead crowd about us when we awake in the morning. . . . Now arises the uneasy question: How can all of this be accommodated in one day? When will I do this, when that? . . . Thus agitated, we would like to run around and rush forth. We must then take the reins in hand and say, "Take it easy! Not any of this may touch me now. My first morning's hour belongs to the Lord. I will tackle the day's work which he charges me with, and he will give me the power to accomplish it."[43]

Giving the Lord the first fruitful moments of our day is still a good idea.

Good morning, Lord!

OCTOBER 26

*And you became imitators of us and of the Lord, receiving
the word in great affliction, with joy from the holy Spirit, so
that you became a model for all the believers.*

1 Thessalonians 1:6-7

It's OK to fake it until you make it, as the saying goes. Early in
my career, my boss told me that I had to present a daylong
training to my coworkers. I had never even done an hour-long
training before, let alone an entire day. I was terrified. She
seemed unconcerned with my lack of experience, and when
I told her I was scared, she said, "Just do it."

The only way I found the courage to proceed was to pre-
tend that I knew what I was doing. I "acted" my way through
the entire day, imitating the techniques of other workshop
presenters. I learned that not only could I do the training,
but I enjoyed it *and* was good at it.

Lesson learned.

Lord, let me become a good imitator of you.

OCTOBER 27

He reached down from on high and seized me;
drew me out of the deep waters.
Psalm 18:17

A long with discovering I could fake it till I make it, here is something else I've discovered: sometimes the only way to get to solid ground is to jump off a cliff. Our fears are going to be with us whether we hunker down or take a leap of faith. We might as well go for it and take the leap, fears and all. Fears are feelings; they are not facts. The facts are that we can do a lot more than we think we can, even when we're afraid.

During the free falls of life, God's rescuing arm is ready to steady us. Go ahead and take the plunge.

Lord, I'm ready.

OCTOBER 28

But grace was given to each of us according to the measure
of Christ's gift.
Ephesians 4:7

Your goal is not to be liked, but to be holy. Whether you are dealing with your children, your coworkers, or your extended family, your responsibility is to be as holy as you can be through the grace that you have been given. The Litany of Humility can help us as we look for ways to grow in this virtue:

That others may be loved more than I,
[Response] Jesus, grant me the grace to desire it.
That others may be esteemed more than I . . .
That, in the opinion of the world,
others may increase and I may decrease . . .
That others may be chosen and I set aside . . .
That others may be praised and I unnoticed . . .
That others may be preferred to me in everything . . .
That others may become holier than I, provided that I may
become as holy as I should . . .[44]

Pray this and you will be well on your way to reaching the goal.

Lord, make me holy.

OCTOBER 29

Entrust your works to the LORD,
and your plans will succeed.
Proverbs 16:3

Jolene explained that she used to have to "get nervous in order to get motivated." She would wait until the last minute to start a project because when she let her fretting fuel her procrastination, it supported her idea she needed to be under pressure in order to get things done. With the help of a good counselor, she unraveled this false scenario and achieved a vision of something better.

Instead of being motivated by nervous energy, Jolene envisioned herself as calm, confident, and collected as she began a project. She learned to value and build in ample preparation time as vital to ensuring the best possible outcome. She taught herself to approach her work and responsibilities with serenity, knowing that doing a good job was something she had time for. She now had the ability to accomplish her goals without unnecessary angst.

Lord, purify my motivations.

OCTOBER 30

"And your Father who sees in secret will repay you."
Matthew 6:4

A magnet on my refrigerator says, "Act as if what you do makes a difference. It does." It's a good reminder that what we do has repercussions, either good or bad, even if no one is watching. And today's verse reminds us that God is always watching! Remember, though, that God isn't watching so that he can catch you doing something wrong, but so that he can reward you for doing something right. He's not looking to condemn you; he wants to celebrate the goodness in you.

Lord, see me.

OCTOBER 31

*"And how does this happen to me, that the mother of my
Lord should come to me?"*
Luke 1:43

One of my favorite images of Mary is a life-size bronze statue
by the artist Jim Gion for St. Mary Church in Albany,
Oregon. Titled *Madonna*, it's a breathtaking depiction of her
with her arms outstretched, palms up, stepping out toward the
world. Her body language can be interpreted in many ways,
but when I first saw it, I experienced it as the embodiment of
her open heart welcoming us as her children. She looks as if
she is going to give a mama-bear hug to the world.

A few years later, I viewed it again and felt that she was send-
ing me forth to share her Son with the world. Mary's motherly
embrace is like that. She draws us near and sends us forth at
the same time. Her love doesn't control—it conceives, creates,
and calls us forth as her beloved little ones. What a perfect
mother we have!

Mother Mary, I love you.

NOVEMBER

NOVEMBER 1

ALL SAINTS' DAY

He who consecrates and those who are being consecrated all have one origin. Therefore, he is not ashamed to call them "brothers."

Hebrews 2:11

We are called to be saints, but most of us feel we fall far short of that mark. We're discouraged, in part because we think of the saints as perfect. They weren't. They are those who let God bring his love to perfection within and through them. In the process, they practiced heroic virtue, but they achieved sanctity step-by-step, the same way we do.

Today we celebrate the communion of saints, those who are in heaven in full union with God. These men, women, and children who have gone before us are not resting on their laurels, however. They are our friends who intercede for those of us still on earth, battling our way to heaven.

When we ask our heavenly helpers to pray for us, they bring our requests to God. Go team!

Lord, thank you for your saints.

NOVEMBER 2

ALL SOULS' DAY

For if we believe that Jesus died and rose, so too will God, through Jesus, bring with him those who have fallen asleep.
1 Thessalonians 4:14

Today we remember all the faithful departed who have left this world and are in purgatory. The souls in purgatory continue to be part of our family; therefore, just as we pray for our loved ones on earth, we continue to pray for them, as well as for all the holy souls with them, when they die. We can ask their prayers for us as well. Anyone who has lost a loved one knows that we continue to love them and relate to them, but in a different way.

Today, reflect on the good memories you have of those who have gone before you. If you had a difficult relationship with a person when they were alive, your prayers may be even more meaningful now to help them get to heaven.

Lord, bless our souls.

NOVEMBER 3

They that hope in the LORD will renew their strength,
they will soar on eagles' wings;
They will run and not grow weary,
walk and not grow faint.
Isaiah 40:31

A priest remarked in a homily that the Lord *expects* us to wait. Consider that Noah waited 120 years for rain, Abraham and Sara waited 25 years for a child, Moses waited 40 years in the desert, and even Jesus waited 30 years to begin his life's work. What are you waiting for? God has a unique purpose and plan—some way that he will act in your life—as you wait.

I waited seven years to conceive my child, and I am currently in the twenty-second year of waiting for something that I desire with all my heart. In both circumstances, I can see the way God has worked within me. Waiting is rarely fun, but it can be fruitful. God may have something to teach us beyond a lesson in patience. Be open and let him renew you with his strength.

Lord, help me to not grow weary in waiting.

NOVEMBER 4

"My grace is sufficient for you, for power is made
perfect in weakness."
2 Corinthians 12:9

God uses our most difficult struggles to bring about our greatest strengths. If you have a repeated sin or challenge that you cannot overcome, you are enduring the trial of your own weakness for a reason.

One man struggled with feelings of inferiority. As a result, he developed a critical nature and a spirit of perfectionism that drove people away. No matter how much he tried to change, he was never the person that he wanted to be. One day in the confessional, a priest asked him how he thought God's power could be made perfect in this seemingly perpetual weakness.

By grace, the man made peace with his weaknesses, accepting himself as fallible and imperfect. Consequently, he became much more compassionate. Instead of condemning others, he embraced a deep empathy for them and their ongoing struggles.

Over time, his life became full of friendships with people who were drawn to him because they could trust him with their pain.

Lord, use my weakness.

NOVEMBER 5

Taste and see that the Lord is good; blessed is the stalwart one who takes refuge in him.

Psalm 34:9

We all have a hunger inside. Spiritually speaking, it is our deep desire for complete union with God. Psychologically, it is yearning for wholeness, safe attachment, and peace of mind. Physically, hunger prompts us to nourish our bodies so that we are healthy and strong.

Is it any wonder that Jesus made himself bread and called himself the "Bread of Life"? He wants to be our sustenance on every level. At Mass, Jesus pours himself out as we take our place at the banquet table that transforms and saves us. Author Scott Hahn says, "We go to heaven when we go to Mass."[45]

Jesus says, "Behold, I stand at the door and knock. If anyone hears my voice and opens the door, [then] I will enter his house and dine with him, and he with me" (Revelation 3:20). The message is clear: we have to open the door in order to let Jesus in. Acknowledging our hunger is the first step.

Lord, satisfy my hungry heart.

NOVEMBER 6

For God did not give us a spirit of cowardice but rather
of power and love and self-control.
2 Timothy 1:7

Applying today's verse to our lives is like activating a super-power. Let's examine these gifts of power, love, and self-control.

A spirit of power: this means that we will be effective. In areas of our lives in which we feel impotent, stuck, or weak, God will empower, equip, and supply a source of strength that is appropriate for the situation.

A spirit of love: we are told that love "bears all things, believes all things, hopes all things, endures all things. / Love never fails" (1 Corinthians 13:7-8). When we receive the spirit of love, we are assured of success in loving others with God's love.

A spirit of self-control: this is called self-discipline or sound mind in some versions of the Bible. It's that quality that enables us to receive grace when we're under pressure and keep our passions under the control of our Spirit-led will.

Holy Spirit, give me a spirit of power, love, and self-control!

NOVEMBER 7

For the grace of God has appeared, . . . training us to reject
godless ways and worldly desires and to live temperately,
justly, and devoutly in this age.
Titus 2:11, 12

Before the fall, Adam and Eve experienced a perfect harmony of intellect, will, and desire, but we do not. Our desires can run amok, our wills can be compromised, and our intellect can be dulled and derailed by sin.

But virtue comes to the rescue. Temperance "moderates the desire for pleasure."[46] God wants us to experience pleasure, physically and spiritually, but he asks that we practice moderation, harmony, and balance in order to regulate and relate in a healthy way to our desires.

Temperance works in concert with fortitude to enable us to keep our fears in perspective. Fortitude "controls rashness and fear in the face of the major pains that threaten to unbalance human nature."[47]

Growing in virtue will help us grow in inner peace and the harmony that God intends for all of us.

Holy Spirit, enlighten and guide me in the way of virtue.

NOVEMBER 8

"Be on guard, so that your hearts will not be weighted down with . . . the worries of life, and that day will not come on you suddenly like a trap."
Luke 21:34 (NASB)

During the month of November, many of us focus on thankfulness in anticipation of the holiday season. We might simultaneously begin to brace for the stress that can come from reconnecting with extended family and the pressure to be joyful and accommodating, no matter how we feel inside. We can get an edge on all this by beginning to prepare our hearts and minds now.

Envision a seesaw. On one side are all the things that warm your heart with gratitude: fond memories, people you love, possessions and provisions that God has given you. On the other side are the worries, anxieties, past traumas, and difficult relationships. In the middle, balancing everything, is Jesus. You're right there with him.

While we shouldn't deny that there may be cause for stress, we can control how much weight we give it on any given day.

Lord, keep me grateful.

NOVEMBER 9

Then Jesus said to his disciples, "Whoever wishes to come after me must deny himself, take up his cross, and follow me."

Matthew 16:24

The world tells us that to be truly happy, we must indulge ourselves until we are full, but Jesus says that we must deny ourselves until we are empty. We're not called to emptiness for its own sake, as in some Eastern philosophies, but so that we can be filled with the Holy Spirit and the graces and gifts that Jesus wants to give us.

Our preoccupation with self can fill us to overflowing—and not in a good way. Eucharistic Adoration is one of the best methods for removing the world from within us. As you sit before the Lord, ask him if you can exchange your worldly cares for his divine intentions for your day. You may not feel different when you do, but you'll be empowered to carry your cross. You'll be filled up with what you need in order to follow him.

Lord, fill me.

NOVEMBER 10

For our struggle is not with flesh and blood but with . . . the world rulers of this present darkness, with the evil spirits in the heavens.

Ephesians 6:12

We can and do have authority in Christ Jesus over the strongholds and spiritual forces that keep us stuck. This authority is strengthened through our participation in the sacraments of the Church, especially Reconciliation and the Eucharist. In these, we receive the power to renounce fear and resist temptations in our daily lives.

The power of love to dispel evil is a proven fact. When we pray the Our Father and say, "Deliver us from evil," let us claim this prayer and believe it for ourselves and for those we love.

Lord, set me free from unnecessary fears and protect me from evil. I take authority over all that keeps me in bondage, specifically _____.

NOVEMBER 11

*So shall my word be / that goes forth from my mouth; /
It shall not return to me empty, / but shall do what pleases
me, / achieving the end for which I sent it.*

Isaiah 55:11

Taking life one day at a time is a good idea, but sometimes
an entire day is too hard to contend with. There have been
times in my life when I had to take it five minutes at a time. On
those days, the word of God was my anchor. There is power in
the word of God. Some of my life-rope verses have been:

> He delivered me from passing to the pit, / and my life sees
> light. (Job 33:28)
> Even though I walk through the valley of the shadow of
> death, / I will fear no evil, for you are with me; / your rod
> and your staff comfort me. (Psalm 23:4)
> He is like a tree / planted near streams of water, / that yields
> its fruit in season; / Its leaves never wither; whatever he does
> prospers. (Psalm 1:3)

Whatever the fear is, name it; find a Scripture verse and
hold onto it.

Lord, I love your word.

NOVEMBER 12

But I, like an olive tree flourishing in the house of God,
I trust in God's mercy forever and ever.
Psalm 52:10

Olive trees are uniquely beautiful, but they're not majestic like the redwood or mighty oak. They're not adorned with colorful leaves in the fall like the maple or aspen. In fact, they are squatty, gnarly, and often shallow rooted. Still, they can grow anywhere, under any kind of condition, and some have been around for thousands of years. You can't easily kill an olive tree.

That's why the psalmist compared himself to one. His tenacious trust mimics the olive tree's steadfastness and ability to survive in any kind of weather. We flourish in God's house, and in our lives, when we trust him against all odds. Trust is an act of the will. Even if our roots are shallow, when we wrap them around the firm foundation of our trust in God, we won't just survive—we'll thrive.

Lord, I trust in you.

NOVEMBER 13

"Therefore I tell you, do not worry about your life."
Matthew 6:25

Today is the memorial of St. Frances Xavier Cabrini, also known as Mother Cabrini. She was canonized in 1946, the first naturalized citizen of the United States to be declared a saint. For those of us who struggle with anxiety, she offers this prayer:

> Fortify me with the grace of your Holy Spirit and give your peace to my soul that I may be free from all needless anxiety, solicitude and worry. Help me to desire always that which is pleasing and acceptable to you so that your Will may be my will. Grant that I may rid myself of all unholy desires and that, for your love, I may remain obscure and unknown in this world, to be known only to you. Do not permit me to attribute to myself the good that you perform in me and through me, but rather, referring all honor to your Majesty, may I glory only in my infirmities, so that renouncing sincerely all vainglory which comes from the world, I may aspire to that true and lasting glory which comes from you.[48]

Amen!

NOVEMBER 14

For by the grace given to me I tell everyone among you not to think of himself more highly than one ought to think, but to think soberly, each according to the measure of faith that God has apportioned.

Romans 12:3

Learning to trust ourselves is an important life lesson of adulthood, the fruit of our growing self-knowledge. Trusting ourselves is an act of humility because it means we're aware of our imperfections but remain willing to take appropriate risks when necessary.

St. Teresa of Calcutta explained it like this: "Self-knowledge puts us on our knees, and it is very necessary for love. For knowledge of God produces love, and knowledge of self produces humility."[49]

Do you need to grow in trusting yourself? Take time to reflect on how you can.

Lord, teach me to trust.

NOVEMBER 15

And the one who searches hearts knows what is the intention of the Spirit, because it intercedes for the holy ones according to God's will.

Romans 8:27

Kathryn worries that she doesn't pray "hard enough." She wonders if God will answer her prayers when she gets distracted or when her prayers aren't long and flowing. But God isn't judging the quality of our prayers. He hears us with his heart.

St. Thérèse of Lisieux, who sometimes fell asleep during prayer, wrote, "For me, prayer is a surge of the heart; it is a simple look turned toward heaven, it is a cry of recognition and of love, embracing both trial and joy."[50]

Prayer is not performance; it's a conversation. Grab a cup of your favorite warm drink and pray.

Lord, listen up!

NOVEMBER 16

The one who supplies seed to the sower and bread for food
will supply and multiply your seed and increase the harvest
of your righteousness.
2 Corinthians 9:10

*R*elease, surrender, abandon, detach. These words are the spiritual root system against fear and anxiety. They describe
an interior state of being that we want to achieve. So how do
we get there?

Start by determining which one of the words resonates
with you. My personal favorite is *abandon*. *Surrender* feels as if
I'm giving up, but *abandon* implies that I'm leaving my worries and anxious thoughts in the dust. Some people like the
word *release* because it reminds them of flying and freedom,
as though they're releasing balloons or doves of peace.

Ask yourself, "Which of these words germinates a vision in
my mind or feeling in my heart?" Take time today to reflect
on the word that inspires you the most. Plant it in your heart.
It will blossom come harvest time.

Lord, help me plant freedom in my heart.

NOVEMBER 17

The Lord is with me to the end.
Psalm 138:8

The sign in front of the church read, "Fear has two meanings: forget everything and run, or face everything and rise." No matter what confronts us, we always have a choice to face the situation or flee. Psychologists call this the fight-or-flight response. When we stay put and face what we fear, there is hope that we can resolve the situation or at least put it in perspective so that we can proceed unencumbered. When we flee from life's troubles and threats, however, we'll still need to deal with them down the line because avoiding them only prolongs the inevitable.

Is there a difficult relationship, a struggle, or some other situation you need to face? Maybe you "took flight" a long time ago or are tempted to now. If you need courage, ask God for it. If you need forgiveness, confess and receive absolution. If you need clarity, the Holy Spirit can provide it.

Fear does not have to be your legacy or your default mode. Sometimes you have to fight for peace.

Lord, help me face my fears.

NOVEMBER 18

This is the will of God, your holiness.
1 Thessalonians 4:3

We are all a work in progress. What we perceive as our failures can be our stepping-stones to greatness in the Lord. Remember the story of Peter and his men who were out fishing all night but caught nothing? (see Luke 5:1-10). Jesus instructed them to "put out into deep water" and cast their nets again (5:4). Peter didn't understand, but he obeyed anyway, and the result was beyond successful. Clearly, Peter and his men could not have done it on their own. Their fishing failure turned into success because they obeyed.

We can be holy because God is holy. When we let him work through us, live in us, and show us how to love, we will accomplish things for his kingdom that we never thought possible. You can do his will. Give him your limitations and see what God can do.

Lord, complete me.

NOVEMBER 19

Whatever you do, do from the heart, as for the Lord and not for others, knowing that you will receive from the Lord the due payment of the inheritance.
Colossians 3:23-24

Maybe, like many people, you have a love/hate relationship with your workplace. Even if you love your job, it can still be a source of tremendous stress. You need to be at peak performance, whether you feel like it or not, and you have to deal with different personalities and daily challenges.

Nevertheless, we learn some of our best life lessons at work. Work has taught me that even when I make a mistake, I have value, and that difficult people are difficult because they're afraid to fail. What has work taught you?

Whatever we do, if we do it for love of Jesus, we're going to be successful. The fruit of our efforts will flourish beyond the task at hand. In approaching our jobs as co-laborers with Jesus, we bring great dignity to our work no matter how rewarding or challenging our workplaces might be.

Lord, receive my work.

NOVEMBER 20

I . . . urge you to live in a manner worthy of the call you have received.

Ephesians 4:1

It's important to seek a good fit between your talents, temperament, and job. You won't always have the luxury of a perfect match, but it's an exercise in humility to know your strengths and weaknesses and work within them. You can't do everything.

For many years during my career, I was driven by a need for approval. As a result, I tried to be good at everything. I didn't take the time to discern my true vocation or figure out how to apply my gifts in the workplace. Consequently, I always felt like I was a square peg in a round hole. No wonder I was anxious!

I was trying to force competence where I had very little, and I was failing to fully develop areas where I had natural ability. Freedom came the day I was able to say, "I'm sorry, but I don't know how to do that." I was then able to focus on what I could do.

Lord, help me live and work worthily.

NOVEMBER 21

His divine power has bestowed on us everything that makes
for life and devotion.
2 Peter 1:3

D o you need a prescription for living? Do you need a boost?
St. Peter delivers a step-by-step remedy in his second letter. It goes like this:

> Make every effort to supplement your faith with virtue, virtue
> with knowledge, knowledge with self-control, self-control with
> endurance, endurance with devotion, devotion with mutual
> affection, mutual affection with love. (2 Peter 1: 5-7)

God gives us the power to apply each one of these steps to
our lives. Practice makes for progress that can eventually lead
to perfection in him.

Lord, infuse me with your divine power.

NOVEMBER 22

Trust in the LORD and do good
that you may dwell in the land and live secure.
Psalm 37:3

The connection between doing good and feeling good cannot be denied. Feeling insecure is part of the human condition, but living secure, as today's verse says, is an unshakable experience of confidence. It comes from trusting the Lord's goodness in our lives, regardless of the circumstances, and sharing that goodness with others.

How do we do this? By exercising the supernatural power of grace and choosing to do good despite how others treat us. When we do this, we become overcomers and warriors in the Spirit. Jesus told us that we are to love our enemies. Our arsenal of love includes mercy, speaking the truth, treating others the way that we want to be treated, praying for them, and forgiving them their trespasses. Remember, "perfect love drives out fear" (1 John 4:18).

Lord, equip us to love perfectly.

NOVEMBER 23

Find your delight in the Lord
who will give you your heart's desire.
Psalm 37:4

What is your heart's desire? Have you shared it with the Lord? Of course, he already knows what it is, but if you don't, ask him to reveal it to you. Most of us go through life tamping down our desires. Some of them do need to be tempered and purified, but sometimes in the process, we deaden them all. God doesn't want this.

He gave you emotions so that you can feel deeply, he gave you your senses so that you can experience fully, and he gave you your heart so that you can live abundantly. Delight is a uniquely human experience made possible through divine inspiration. Seek and find your delight in Jesus today.

Lord, I delight in you!

NOVEMBER 24

"Rejoicing in the LORD is your strength!"
Nehemiah 8:10

Helen Keller, who was both blind and deaf and obviously didn't have an easy life, said, "What really counts in life is the quiet meeting of every difficulty with the determination to get out of it all the good there is."[51] She would agree with my dad, who said, "If something is worth doing, it's worth sweating and fretting over." The bottom line is that we have to put in the work to get the reward.

In times of struggle, when trials overwhelm us and when we've reached the end of our rope, we can repeat today's verse like a mantra. It will help to get us through. We're not going to feel joyful all the time, but the Lord's joy can be our strength as we get the job done.

Lord, be my strength.

NOVEMBER 25

"Leave it for this year also, and I shall cultivate the ground around it and fertilize it."
Luke 13:8

In the parable of the fig tree (see Luke 13:6-9), the vineyard owner has all but given up on a tree that has not borne fruit for three years. He threatens to uproot it. The caretaker, though, asks for one more year to tend it in order to bring forth the best in it. In this parable, the owner is God, the caretaker is Jesus, and we are the fig tree.

Jesus aims to help us cultivate our gifts. This involves digging up the weeds of worry that can stunt our growth, as well as daily pruning. He "fertilizes" us with his word and the sacraments. Our super food is his Body and Blood. Jesus is the patient gardener of our hearts. Sometimes his weeding and tending can be painful, but it's always worthwhile when we consider the beautiful bloom he's cultivating. What work do you and Jesus need to do to bring out the best in you?

Lord, cultivate me.

NOVEMBER 26

My mouth shall be filled with your praise,
shall sing your glory every day.
Psalm 71:8

We have the opportunity every day to give thanks and praise to God. As the saying goes, "Our lives are a gift from God—what we do with them is our gift back to him." Here is a beautiful daily offering prayer from St. Thérèse:

O my God ! I offer you all my actions of this day for the intentions and for the glory of the Sacred Heart of Jesus. I desire to sanctify every beat of my heart, my every thought, my simplest works, by uniting them to His infinite merits; and I wish to make reparation for my sins by casting them into the furnace of His Merciful Love.

O my God! I ask of You for myself and for those dear to me, the grace to fulfill perfectly your Holy Will, to accept for love of You the joys and sorrows of this passing life, so that we may one day be united together in Heaven for all eternity. Amen.[52]

Amen, Lord, amen!

NOVEMBER 27

So we are ambassadors for Christ, as if God were appealing through us.
2 Corinthians 5:20

An ambassador is someone who is authorized to represent someone else. You are an ambassador for Christ, according to today's verse—God has authorized you to represent him here in the world. When you are feeling inadequate, insecure, or overwhelmed by what you have to do, stop for a moment and consider your role as an ambassador. You're representing God, and if you let him guide you, he will make his presence known through you.

I once had to teach a classroom full of kindergartners, a task that was very much out of my comfort zone. My prayer of preparation went like this: "Lord, you're going to have to do this because I can't! Let them experience you, not me." Little did I know that I was praying to be an ambassador.

Lord, live through me.

NOVEMBER 28

"Be merciful, just as [also] your Father is merciful."
Luke 6:36

Check in with the "mercy meter" today. How merciful have you been lately—to yourself and others? God has described himself, above all, as merciful. To be most like him, we need to be as well. Do you need to replace a harsh inner critic with a merciful mentor? Do you need to cut others some slack, let them off the hook, and accept them, imperfections and all?

Mercy leads to peace. It puts to rest unrealistic expectations and replaces them with healthy acceptance. It allows God's perfect justice to prevail.

Lord, have mercy.

NOVEMBER 29

Yet the world and its enticement are passing away.
But whoever does the will of God remains forever.
1 John 2:17

Letting go is a lifelong lesson. A clenched fist and a closed heart cannot receive God's grace fully. The things of this world, the possessions and positions we hold so dear, will all pass away.

I had the great honor and blessing of being with my mother in the very last moments of her life here on earth. It was then that I learned how all the things that seemed to matter so much really didn't. In the end, it was just the two of us and the love that God had nurtured between us, despite our personal failings and humanness . . . or maybe because of them.

If we must hold on to anything, let it be hope—hope that our souls and the souls of those we love will remain forever in God.

Lord, teach me.

NOVEMBER 30

He said to them, "Come away by yourselves to a deserted place and rest a while."
Mark 6:31

In the midst of the clamoring crowds pressing in from all sides, desperate for miracles and the attention of Jesus and his apostles, Jesus offered an unlikely suggestion. He told his twelve friends to step aside, go off by themselves, and rest. It seems counterintuitive, but as we enter the busiest season of the year with all its demands, we should do the same.

This is what the Church, in her wisdom, invites us to do through the Advent season. Advent is meant to be a time of silence, preparation, austerity, and calm. Let's carry the spirit of Advent in our hearts in the coming weeks. Is there a heavenly helper who can accompany you as you step aside and rest? Jesus, Mary, or Joseph? Who among the communion of saints can help you get to the heart of this season? Consider choosing a guide to walk with you in the simple beauty and quiet joy of Advent.

Lord, help me to rest.

DECEMBER

DECEMBER 1

So turn from youthful desires and pursue righteousness,
faith, love, and peace, along with those who call on the
Lord with purity of heart.
2 Timothy 2:22

The *Catechism* says that "chastity is a moral virtue. It is also a
gift from God, a *grace*, a fruit of spiritual effort. The Holy
Spirit enables one whom the water of Baptism has regenerated
to imitate the purity of Christ" (2345). God knew that chastity
would be challenging for us, so he gave us Mary, the perfect
model of this virtue. She embodies the physical, emotional,
and spiritual chastity to which God calls us.

St. Josemaría Escrivá reminded us of the powerful intercession that Mary brings:

> So your strength is failing you? Why don't you tell your mother
> about it? . . . Mother! Call her with a loud voice. She is listen-
> ing to you; she sees you in danger, perhaps, and she—your holy
> mother Mary—offers you, along with the grace of her son, the
> refuge of her arms, the tenderness of her embrace . . . and you
> will find yourself with added strength for the new battle.[53]

Mother, help me now!

DECEMBER 2

Do not fear, you shall not be put to shame;
do not be discouraged, you shall not be disgraced.
Isaiah 54:4

It's been said that every saint has a past and every sinner has a future. Just so, most of us have done things we're not proud of. Some of us, though, are haunted by our mistakes and unable to shake the shame and guilt associated with them. We begin to view life through the lens of our failures, letting the devil jump in and mire us in shame.

God doesn't want us to wallow in shame or despair. Instead, he wants to restrain and purify the effects of shame on our hearts. In other words, he wants to put shame and the devil in their place. Will we let him?

Lord, purify me.

DECEMBER 3

What you decide shall succeed for you,
and upon your ways light shall shine.
Job 22:28

The pressure to live up to worldly expectations for a perfect Christmas can weigh heavily on us at this time of year. Anita was struggling with the anxiety provoked by this tension when her friend suggested that she suspend all expectations and just enjoy each moment as it came. Anita was skeptical, but she gave it a try. The first thing she did was to list all the unspoken hopes and plans that were weighing on her. She discovered that some of the ideas were unrealistic, and others were impossible. She'd never be able to do it all. She decided to let go of the expectations altogether and replace them with a few practical action steps for the season. They were

1) I will treat myself with kindness and compassion.
2) I will not be offended by the actions or inactions of others.
3) I will make time for silence and Jesus every day.

What would be on your list?

Lord, settle me.

DECEMBER 4

Beloved, do not trust every spirit but test the spirits to see whether they belong to God.

1 John 4:1

The world is full of confusion and duplicity, but God has given the Church everything it needs to discern what is "the will of God, what is good and pleasing and perfect" (Romans 12:2).

Let's not look to the world for answers, but rather, let us enter into the depths of our hearts, pondering the word of God. We might need to consult a trained spiritual director, priest, deacon, or religious to guide us. The Church also offers many different forms of spirituality—Carmelite, Ignatian, or Benedictine, for example—to help us discern what is good and true.

Instead of remaining in confusion, we can use all the tried-and-true methods of the Church to test the spirits.

Lord, show me the way.

DECEMBER 5

*You should put away the old self . . . , and put on the new
self, created in God's way in righteousness and
holiness of truth.*

Ephesians 4:22, 24

Today's verse inspires an interesting question: if you were
put on trial for being a Christian, would there be enough
evidence to convict you? If you know Jesus, has he made a difference in your life? Is there a "before and after" version of
you? Have you received his power and presence in order to
change for the better?

What is it that you need to lay aside? Worry, fear, a need
to control? Do you need deliverance from a sin that seems to
cling to you? You were made to be like God. He sent Jesus into
the world so that we could always hope for more. Let it be so.

Lord, make me new.

DECEMBER 6

"Prepare the way of the Lord, / make straight his paths."
Mark 1:3

Wait, listen, stay awake, prepare, stop what you are doing, and look up. These are the action steps of Advent. Each is an invitation from the Lord to help us receive him more fully. Which action speaks to your heart? Are you being invited to wait? Have you embraced the silence of the season? Have you tuned your spirit into the heavenly realm? Are you making room for Jesus in your life? Is your focus on Jesus?

Of all the activities of the season, the ones that lead us closer to Jesus are the most important and the ones we should pursue.

Lord, I am ready to receive you.

DECEMBER 7

"Mary has chosen the better part and it will not be taken from her."
Luke 10:42

Just when I think I have perfectionism beat, it rears its ugly head. It happened again after spending all afternoon preparing food for a holiday party. When my family didn't arrive on schedule, my precisely choreographed meal fell flat and grew cold. You can guess what happened next.

Instead of welcoming them joyfully when they finally did arrive, I greeted them with exasperation and annoyance because my beautiful meal was no more. I could almost hear Jesus, saying, "Martha, Martha, you are anxious and worried about many things" (Luke 10:41).

Still, I have come a long way in my battle with perfectionism, a trait that is very different from excellence. Perfectionism values performance over people. Excellence, while striving for the best, accepts our limitations and those of others.

Pride fuels perfectionism. Letting go of it has allowed me to embrace the spirit of Mary and choose "the better part."

Lord, deliver me from me!

DECEMBER 8

THE FEAST OF THE IMMACULATE CONCEPTION
I will put enmity between you and the woman, / and between your offspring and hers; / They will strike at your head, / while you strike at their heel.
Genesis 3:15

In an article about the Immaculate Conception of Mary, Fr. William G. Most wrote,

> The Catholic Church teaches that from the very moment of her conception, the Blessed Virgin Mary was free from all stain of original sin. This simply means that from the beginning, she was in a state of grace, sharing in God's own life, and that she was free from the sinful inclinations which have beset human nature after the fall.[54]

By God's design, Mary is perfect. His plan for our redemption incudes her, as we see in today's verse that references her role in the battle over evil. We don't usually think of Mary as fierce, but she is. Her strength is unmatched among the saints. May we follow in her footsteps and celebrate her perfection today and always.

Mary, be my strength.

DECEMBER 9

Whoever confers benefits will be amply enriched,
and whoever refreshes others will be refreshed.
Proverbs 11:25

Generosity is a healing balm for the soul and a prominent trait of St. Nicholas, whose feast we celebrate today. Most of us need to become more generous. We may need to give more of our time, attention, or talent, without expecting anything in return. We may need to give more of our money or material possessions in order to advance the kingdom of God.

The story of the widow's mite (see Mark 12:41-44) shows us that we don't have to be rich to be generous; we just need to be willing to give. How are you being called to be generous in this season of giving?

Lord, create a generous heart within me.

DECEMBER 10

*As each one has received a gift, use it to serve one another
as good stewards of God's varied grace.*
1 Peter 4:10

The pressure we feel to buy the perfect gift can squelch the joy of giving that springs naturally out of the presence of the Giver in our hearts. If we think back, the best gifts we've received are most likely the homemade ornaments, the candlelit dinner cooked from scratch, or the spontaneous moment of joy captured with those we love.

We don't remember *things* as much as we treasure *experiences*. God's grace lives in the simple pleasures of our lives. Being a good steward means we don't squander those experiences or worry them away, but instead savor the gift of each priceless moment.

Lord, gift me with your grace.

DECEMBER 11

He is not the God of disorder but of peace.
1 Corinthians 14:33

Keep it simple. Confusion is not of God. When our imagination takes us down the treacherous path of deep thoughts that lead nowhere, this is not God's doing.

The Holy Spirit brings clarity and enlightenment. A life lived in and for Christ is marked by order and singleness of heart. Our direction and responsibilities are straightforward.

> What the LORD requires of you:
> Only to do justice and to love goodness,
> and to walk humbly with your God. (Micah 6:8)

Simplicity does take effort, but it's worth it.

Holy Spirit, clear the way.

DECEMBER 12

OUR LADY OF GUADALUPE

"Blessed is the womb that carried you."

Luke 11:27

There's nothing like the comfort of a loving mother's words. Here are Mary's beautiful words to Juan Diego when she appeared to him in Guadalupe, Mexico:

> Listen, put it into your heart, . . . that the thing that disturbs you, the thing that afflicts you, is nothing. Do not let your . . . heart be disturbed. Do not fear this sickness . . . nor anything that is sharp or hurtful. Am I not here, I, who am your Mother? Are you not under my shadow and protection? Am I not the source of your joy? Are you not in the hollow of my mantle, in the crossing of my arms? Do you need anything more? Let nothing else worry you, or disturb you.[55]

Mary is your mother. Imagine that she is saying these healing words to you today. Let them sink into your spirit and soothe you.

Mother Mary, blessed are you.

DECEMBER 13

*Do you not know that your body is a temple of the holy
Spirit within you, whom you have from God, and that you
are not your own? . . . Therefore glorify God in your body.*
1 Corinthians 6:19, 20

The body is a gift; it's holy ground. Our struggles with our
body are real, but they are known to Jesus because he too
had a human body. During his lifetime, he experienced what
it was like to be tired, hungry, and tempted. His heart beat
just as ours does. He became incarnate so that he could give
his body as a living sacrifice for us.

We are meant to honor our bodies by our actions and honor
God with our bodies. We do this by embracing our dignity and
remembering that God created the human body. He declared
the body good, and he sanctifies our bodies through his.

Lord, my body is a gift.

DECEMBER 14

For we all fall short in many respects. If anyone does not
fall short in speech, he is a perfect man, able to bridle his
whole body also.

James 3:2

What we say has the potential to kill or to exalt, to destroy
or to raise up. Words are powerful, and they matter. The
Catechism says that chastity is a virtue that not only applies to
what we do, but also to what we say (see 2338). Our words can
get us into a trouble faster than anything else. James refers to
our tongues as fire for this very reason.

If we can discipline our mouths, we will advance in holiness
and happiness. Every time I leave Mass, I dip my fingers in
the holy water, make the Sign of the Cross, and trace an extra
cross on my lips to remind me that I can always use the extra
help when it comes to choosing my words carefully.

Lord, help me keep my words pure.

DECEMBER 15

"The fire on the altar is to be kept burning; it must
not go out."
Leviticus 6:5

In every Catholic Church around the world, a sanctuary lamp burns to signify Christ's presence in the Tabernacle. Surprisingly, as we see in today's verse, this practice as a means of announcing God's presence dates all the way back to the time of Moses. The roots of our faith run deep.

The Church has never been without its challenges and strife. But even though the members of the body of Christ are wounded and broken, in the end the Lord will triumph. Every time that we proclaim our faith or act in Jesus' name, we are strengthening the Church. During this season of light, let's remember that we are part of something bigger than ourselves, a light that cannot be extinguished. Let those of us within the Church believe that Christ is with us and will never forsake us.

Lord, let your light shine.

DECEMBER 16

"For where your treasure is, there also will your heart be."
Matthew 6:21

We are responsible for the way we prioritize our time, energy, and life goals. How we spend our time, what we pour our energy into, and what we focus on reveal what we treasure most. Worrying excessively about something is not treasuring it. If we find that we are fretting or focusing negative attention on something, it may mean we need to examine our priorities.

Think of your heart as a treasure chest. What have you put in it? If you set your heart on God's goodness *first*—his jewels of peace, serenity, and hope—then you will be well equipped to cope with the pressing priorities that surround you.

Lord, you are first in my heart.

DECEMBER 17

For the Lord does not reject forever; . . .
He does not willingly afflict or bring grief to human beings.
Lamentations 3:31, 33

All of us experience times when God seems very far away.
Grief, more than anything, can make us feel alone and
abandoned by him. Try to think of grief as a passing season—
typically winter, when the world is frozen and barren. On the
surface, it seems that spring will never come with its warmth
and beauty, but it always does. The rebirth in our souls that
follows grieving is like the arrival of a rich and welcome springtime. After the thaw, the blooms seem to have a unique beauty.
You can't force them.

Especially at this time of year, honor grief, and hold fast
to the fact that the Master Gardener has planted seeds of joy
that will bloom in season.

Lord, tend my soul.

DECEMBER 18

"I command you: be strong and steadfast! Do not fear nor be dismayed, for the LORD, your God, is with you wherever you go."
Joshua 1:9

Letting go of our fears is not just a good idea; it's a direct order from God. If God is our constant companion, then we don't need our fears to protect us. In order to be strong and steadfast, we need his confidence cruising through our veins. He will provide this.

When we remember that God is always with us to help us carry out his commandments, his laws become blessings rather than burdens. They bring us to a better version of who he calls us to be.

Lord, make me strong and steadfast.

DECEMBER 19

*Then [Jesus] made his disciples get into the boat and
precede him to the other side toward Bethsaida, while he
dismissed the crowd.*

Mark 6:45

Self-care is an essential ingredient for the holidays. A recipe for success in surviving the season will include tending to your emotional, spiritual, and physical health. Just as in today's verse, you may need to follow Jesus' lead as you strive to balance your needs with those of others. Self-denial is good for the soul, but you can't give away what you don't have. It's up to you to get what you need to stay sane and embrace the spirit of the season.

Sit down and make a self-care list. It might include using the word *no* more often or putting yourself at the top of the list for grabbing quiet time and a good haircut. Pay attention to your pace and refuse to indulge in guilt over things you can't control.

To be as present as possible to the beauty and wonder of Christ's coming, gift yourself with the self-care you need.

Lord, I need _____.

DECEMBER 20

Now may the Lord of peace himself give you peace at all times in every way.
2 Thessalonians 3:16 (ESV)

God promises us a peace that runs deep. I used to live with a tsunami of fear, but now I am plunged into the depths of his peace. The living waters of his tender mercies are available to all of us. What we long for, we will receive. You don't have to take my word for it because God's word is overflowing with proof of his promises. Believe him. God cannot lie (see Hebrews 6:18). Claim his peace, let it overtake you, and let the waves of worry be washed away by his love.

Lord, rush in.

DECEMBER 21

For we are his handiwork, created in Christ Jesus for the
good works that God has prepared in advance, that we
should live in them.
Ephesians 2:10

We all have a purpose in life, and God equips us to be
successful and fruitful in accomplishing it. He is our
greatest cheerleader and champion. Our good works are *his*
design, but he leaves it up to us to do them. He's at our side—
we don't have to do this alone—but we don't have to compete
for his attention or affirmation either.

We are the work of his hands, beloved and beautiful in
his sight.

Lord, thank you for creating me.

DECEMBER 22

With all vigilance guard your heart,
for in it are the sources of life.
Proverbs 4:23

O ur heart is the center of our being. The *Catechism* says
that our desire for God is written in our heart and that
only in God will we find the truth and happiness that we are
searching for (see 27). What a joy to know that our desire for
God is already within us, written in our hearts where he dwells!

This means we must guard our hearts; we must allow God
to purify our attachments and bring a right order to our affec-
tions. We need to make room for him, clearing out the clutter
of our worn-out worries and letting go of resentments. A crown
of thorns surrounds the image of his Sacred Heart. I like to
think that when we let go of our sins and unforgiveness, it's
as if we're plucking thorns from his heart.

God wants to have a heart-to-heart communion with us.
What do we need to let go of to make that happen?

Lord, cleanse my heart.

DECEMBER 23

Rejoice in the Lord always. I shall say it again: rejoice!
Philippians 4:4

Jesus is coming! Jesus is coming! Are you excited? Our cause for rejoicing is almost here. The joy of this season is meant to be shared all year long. Each time we receive Jesus in the Eucharist, our faces should beam, and our hearts should swell with joy in his presence. Rejoicing is not only a way of feeling, however; it's also an act of love and honor. Welcoming Jesus is not a once-a-year or even a once-a-week event. It's the cry of every beat of our hearts.

Jesus, come!

DECEMBER 24

Surely, the LORD, your God, has blessed you in all your undertakings; he has been concerned about your journey through this vast wilderness.
Deuteronomy 2:7

The journey to Jesus is worth every step. In a sense, we are all on a pilgrimage—a journey undertaken to reflect on God and honor him. On this pilgrimage of life, it helps to keep our heavenly destination in mind. That will give us perspective because sometimes we feel like we're wandering in circles like the Israelites. And sometimes we are, but we can find blessing even there as long as we say at every twist and turn, "Yes, Lord."

Lord, with every step you have my yes.

DECEMBER 25

THE NATIVITY OF THE LORD
Through him was life,
and this life was the light of the human race.
John 1:4

The wisest among us can build great empires and advance great truths, but it took a tiny baby, wrapped in swaddling clothes and born in a manger, to bring the kingdom of God to earth. The gifts of our greatest thinkers, theologians, authors, and saints pale in comparison.

Because of Jesus, the lowliest among us can be great. Because of Jesus, the dead are raised to new life. Because Love broke through the darkness, we can walk in the light.

Let this blessed day and the rest of the Christmas season be a reminder that we are children of the light, created in God's image, beloved and chosen.

Lord, I receive your gift.

DECEMBER 26

You will not abandon me into enemy hands,
but will set my feet in a free and open space.
Psalm 31:9

Today is the feast of St. Stephen, the first martyr of the Church. On the surface, it might seem a downer to celebrate his death in the midst of this season of joy, but Stephen shows us how to be entirely free from worldly concern. Scripture says that he was "filled with grace and power" (Acts 6:8).

Stephen was inspired by a love that delivered him from all his fears, even the fear of suffering and death. While being stoned for his faith, he forgave his persecutors just as Jesus did. He could not possibly have loved his enemies so completely, apart from Jesus. St. Stephen exemplifies the same love and freedom that Jesus offers us when we let him take over our hearts.

Lord, occupy my heart.

DECEMBER 27

"Let the children come to me; do not prevent them, for the
kingdom of God belongs to such as these. Amen, I say to
you, whoever does not accept the kingdom of God like a child
will not enter it.
Mark 10:14-15

Play is essential to the human spirit and it is for all of us
who are God's children, no matter what the age. We need
unstructured leisure and joyful rest. Our souls were created
to drink in the beauty of our surroundings and share in the
intimate embrace of sweet friendships and heart-to-heart
encounters. These are the "sacred pauses" of life when our
hearts are expanded and our imaginations replenished.

Make a "play date" and keep it with the Holy Spirit. How
can he lift you up and fill you? What will speak to your spirit
and feed your soul?

This is your mission: go outside and play!

Lord, ready, set, go!

DECEMBER 28

Remain in me, as I remain in you. Just as a branch cannot
bear fruit on its own unless it remains on the vine,
so neither can you unless you remain in me.
John 15:4

There's a saying, "it is never too late to become who you could have been," and there are many examples to prove it. Famous late bloomers include Mother Teresa, who 47 when she opened her first orphanage; renowned artist Grandma Moses, who didn't pick up a paintbrush until she was 75; and even Jesus, who didn't start his ministry until he was 30. The hope that we have is that God never gives up on us, so why should we? Some seeds take longer to grow. There is even one form of wildflower that only blooms once every 3000 years!' Thankfully, we don't have to wait that long. Through him, with him, and in him, we will bear good fruit.

Lord, help me bloom.

DECEMBER 29

"Joseph, son of David, do not be afraid."
Matthew 1:20

A shout-out to St. Joseph today! No doubt he had many plans for his life that fell by the wayside when he became betrothed to Mary. He could have divorced her quietly when he received news of her pregnancy, but he chose to follow God's plan. And when the angel instructed him to take his family into exile, he didn't hesitate but fled with them "by night" (Matthew 2:14). Joseph's demeanor under pressure and his faithfulness to God have made him a beloved figure and powerful intercessor. His pure desire to do God's will in every circumstance makes him a role model for us all.

St. Joseph, be my guide.

DECEMBER 30

FEAST OF THE HOLY FAMILY

The person who is trustworthy in very small matters is also trustworthy in great ones.

Luke 16:10

Celebrate the little victories, the ones that only Jesus and you know about. It could be a hidden fear conquered, a sharp retort kept quiet, perhaps an inner flutter of the heart toward greater love and healing over a wound that no one ever knew existed. Don't overlook the significance of these quiet triumphs in the hustle and bustle of life. Jesus knows of your efforts and is pleased with your progress. There is no matter so small that he doesn't notice and rejoice with you. Stop, take a moment, and reflect. Savor the small stuff and smile, knowing Jesus is smiling back at you.

Lord, we did it!

DECEMBER 31

There is . . . A time to seek, and a time to lose;
a time to keep, and a time to cast away.
Ecclesiastes 3:6

Sometimes it is hard to let go, to move on, and cast away, especially when things are familiar, comfortable, or secure. But God is always beckoning us forward and inviting us to places that we cannot yet imagine, on our way to the greatest destination of all. We are all in "preparation mode" for better things to come. Every passage that we experience here is part of his plan. Trust it. Trust him; release and receive.

Lord, I'm coming.

NOTES

1. Catholic365.com, in article by Joe Reciniello, June 24, 2016, accessed at http://www.catholic365.com/article/4589/if-you-put-all-the-love-of-all-the-mothers-into-one-heart-it-still-would-not-equal-the-love-of-the-heart-of-mary-for-her-children.html.
2. St. Margaret Mary, *Thoughts and Sayings of St. Margaret Mary* (Charlotte, North Carolina: Tan Books, 1986), Meditation for April 30 (II, 753, 755).
3. Elizabeth A. Mitchell, PhD, *Edith Stein: Seeker of Truth* (Denver: Endow, 2008), 61.
4. ThinkExist.com, "Mother Teresa of Calcutta Quotes," accessed at http://thinkexist.com/quotation/we_can_do_no_great_things-only_small_things_with/11592.html.
5. Goodreads.com, "John Henry Newman Quotes," accessed at http://www.goodreads.com/quotes/408029-god-has-created-me-to-do-him-some -definite-service.
6. EWTN Global Catholic Network, Devotions, "An Act of Spiritual Devotion," accessed at https://www.ewtn.com/devotionals/prayers/blsac4.htm.
7. Wikipedia.org, "Flow (Psychology)," accessed at https://en.wikipedia.org/wiki/Flow_(psychology).
8. Anthony Mottola, *The Spiritual Exercises of St. Ignatius* (Garden City, New York: Image Books, 1964), 130.
9. John A Hardon, SJ, *The Modern Catholic Dictionary* (Inter Mirifica, 1999), accessed at http://www.therealpresence.org/cgi-bin/getdefinition.pl.

10. Our Catholic Prayers, St. Patrick's Breastplate, accessed at https://www.ourcatholicprayers.com/st-patricks-breastplate.html.

11. Tradition in Action, "The Importance of Devotion to St. Joseph," St. Teresa of Avila's Plea accessed at https://www.traditioninaction.org/religious/b008rpJoseph.htm.

12. Catholic Exchange, "How the Saints Faced Anxiety," by Fr. Joseph M. Esper, accessed at https://catholicexchange.com/saints-faced-anxiety.

13. Beliefnet, "Serenity Prayer" by Reinhold Niebuhr (1892-1971), accessed at https://www.beliefnet.com/prayers/protestant/addiction/serenity-prayer.aspx.

14. Bill Johnson Online, "The Other Serenity Prayer," by Eleanor Brownn, accessed at http://billjohnsononline.com/the-other-serenity-prayer/.

15. What Christians Want to Know, "Bible Verses about Patience," accessed at https://www.whatchristianswanttoknow.com/bible-verses-about-patience-20-scripture -quotes/#ixzz5dAKOoX.

16. Jean-Pierre de Caussade, *Abandonment to Divine Providence*, trans. Ella McMahon (New York: Benziger Brothers, 1887), 80, also accessed at https://spiritualdirection.com/2009/06/11/abandonment-xii-finding-the-will-of-god.

17. Christian Classics Ethereal Library, *Dialog of Catherine of Siena*, accessed at https://www.ccel.org/ccel/catherine/dialog.iv.iii.vii.html.

18. Preach It/Teach It.org, "Kindness: Discover the Power of the Forgotten Christian Virtue," Frank Viola, accessed at https://www.preachitteachit.org/articles/detail/kindness-discover-the-power-of-the-forgotten-christian-virtue.

19. Our Catholic Prayers, A Prayer to St. Dymphna, accessed at https://www.ourcatholicprayers.com/prayer-to-st-dymphna.html.

20. Allan McDonald Facebook "Favorite Quotes", Edith Stein, accessed at https://www.facebook.com/allan.macdonald.106.

21. Margaret Mary Alacoque, Quote for the Day: "Abode of the Sacred Heart," accessed at https://saintsworks.net/forums/index.php?action=printpage;topic=1193.0.

22. Neal Lozano, *Resisting the Devil: A Catholic Perspective on Deliverance* (Huntington, IN: Our Sunday Visitor, Inc., 2010), 34.

23. Relevant Magazine, "No, the 'Safest Place' Isn't the Center of God's Will," Corrie ten Boom, accessed at https://relevantmagazine.com/god/no-safest-place-isnt-center-gods-will.

24. John Paul II, New York Times, May 12, 1995, "Pope, on Dutch Trip, Firmly Calls for Church Unity, accessed at https://www.nytimes.com/1985/05/12/world/pope-on-dutch-trip-firmly-calls-for-church-unity.html.

25. Catholic Strength, "Jane Eyre and the Virtue of Heroic Perseverance," accessed at https://catholicstrength.com/tag/longanimity/.

26. Catholic Online, Prayer against Depression, St. Ignatius of Loyola, accessed at https://www.catholic.org/prayers/ prayer.php?p=616.

27. GoodConfession.com, "Growing in Meekness," accessed at https://goodconfession.com/growing-in-meekness/.

28. DifferenceBetween.net, "Difference between Courage and Bravery," accessed at http://www.differencebetween. net/language/difference-between-courage-and-bravery/.

29. Catholicism.org, "Meekness Is Strength, accessed at https://catholicism.org/ad-rem-no-187.html.

30. The Quotations Page, Quotation # 26247, Dr. Thomas Fuller, *Gnomologia*, 1732, accessed at http://www. quotationspage.com/quote/26247.html.

31. Benedict XVI, Encyclical Letter *Spe Salvi* [Saved in Hope], November 30, 2007, 33, accessed at http:// w2.vatican.va/content/benedict-xvi/en/encyclicals/ documents/hf_ben-xvi_enc_20071130_spe-salvi.html.

32. AZ Quotes, Joan of Arc, accessed at https://www. azquotes.com/quote/604387.

33. Our Lady of Mercy Lay Carmelite Community # 565, "St. John of the Cross," accessed at http:// olmlaycarmelites.org/quote/john-cross?page=1.

34. White Lily of the Blessed Trinity, "Quotes about Mary, Mother of God," accessed at http://www. whitelilyoftrinity.com/saints_quotes_mary.html.

35. Aleteia.org, "Humility Is the Source of All Peace," St. John Bosco, accessed at https://aleteia.org/slideshow/15-thoughts-from-the-saints-that-will-make-you-actually -love-humility-2757/3/.

36. St. Maria Faustina Kowalski, *Divine Mercy in My Soul*, (Stockbridge, MA: Association of Marian Fathers, 2007), 459.

37. EWTN Global Catholic Network, "History of the Rosary," Fr. William Saunders, accessed at https://www. ewtn.com/library/ANSWERS/ROSARYHS.HTM.

38. CatholicLink.org, "Rosary Struggles? St. Therese Can Relate," accessed at https://catholic-link.org/quotes/ rosary-struggles-st-therese-can-relate/.

39. Those Catholic Men, "Strategies for Spiritual Warfare," accessed at https://thosecatholicmen.com/articles/ strategies-for-spiritual-warfare/.

40. The Order of Carmelites, "Teresa of Avila Quotes," accessed at https://ocarm.org/en/content/ocarm/teresa-avila-quotes.

41. Viktor Frankl, *Man's Search for Meaning* (Boston: Beacon Press, 2006), 86, accessed at https://www.uky. edu/~eushe2/quotations/frankl.html.

42. The Free Dictionary by Farlex, "Reframing," accessed at https://medical-dictionary.thefreedictionary.com/ reframing.

43. John Sullivan, *Edith Stein: Essential Writings* (Marynoll, NY: Orbis, 2002), 64-65, accessed at https://www. amazon.com/Edith-Stein-Essential-Writings-Spiritual/ dp/1570754284.

44. EWTN Global Catholic Network, Devotions, "Litany of Humility," accessed at https://www.ewtn.com/ Devotionals/prayers/humility.htm.

45. Scott Hahn, *The Lamb's Supper* (New York: Doubleday, 1999), 128.

46. John A. Hardon, SJ, *Catholic Dictionary: An Abridged and Updated Edition of Modern Catholic Dictionary* (New York: Image Press, 1980), 496.

47. Ibid., 496.

48. Aleteia.org, "St. Frances Xavier Cabrini Has Just the Prayer for You," accessed at https://aleteia. org/2018/01/16/stressed-out-pray-this-prayer-to-be-freed-from-needless-anxiety-and-worry/.

49. Aleteia.org, "Slideshow on Humility," accessed at https://aleteia.org/slideshow/15-thoughts-from-the-saints-that-will-make-you-actually-love-humility-2757/5/.

50. The Order of Carmelites, "Therese of Lisieux Quotes," accessed at https://ocarm.org/en/content/ocarm/therese-lisieux-quotes.

51. Helen Keller, *To Love This Life: Quotations by Helen Keller* (New York, NY: American Foundation for the Blind, 2000), 37.

52. Pope's Worldwide Prayer Network, "Daily Offering Prayers," St. Therese of Lisieux's Daily Offering, accessed at http://popesprayerusa.net/daily-offering-prayers/.

53. Josemar a Escrivá, The Way (New York, NY: Image Press, 1982), 88.

54. EWTN Global Catholic Network, Faith and Teaching, "Mary's Immaculate Conception," accessed at https://www.ewtn.com/faith/teachings/marya2.htm.

55. Theotokos.org, "Words Spoken by Mary at Guadalupe," accessed at http://theotokos.org.uk/pages/approved/words/wordguad.html.

the WORD among us ®

The *Spirit* of Catholic Living

This book was published by The Word Among Us. Since 1981, The Word Among Us has been answering the call of the Second Vatican Council to help Catholic laypeople encounter Christ in the Scriptures.

The name of our company comes from the prologue to the Gospel of John and reflects the vision and purpose of all of our publications: to be an instrument of the Spirit, whose desire is to manifest Jesus' presence in and to the children of God. In this way, we hope to contribute to the Church's ongoing mission of proclaiming the gospel to the world so that all people would know the love and mercy of our Lord and grow more deeply in their faith as missionary disciples.

Our monthly devotional magazine, *The Word Among Us*, features meditations on the daily and Sunday Mass readings and currently reaches more than one million Catholics in North America and another half-million Catholics in one hundred countries around the world. Our book division, The Word Among Us Press, publishes numerous books, Bible studies, and pamphlets that help Catholics grow in their faith.

To learn more about who we are and what we publish, visit us at www.wau.org. There you will find a variety of Catholic resources that will help you grow in your faith.

Embrace His Word, Listen to God . . .

www.wau.org